17.50

D1263318

Salvage
Operations

Captain C N T Baptist

STANFORD MARITIME · LONDON

Acknowledgements

The Author would like to thank the following companies and individuals for assistance in providing material and photographs for this book.

The Bureau Wijsmuller, Ijmuiden, Holland.
The Selco Towage and Salvage Company, Singapore.
Exxon Corporation of New York, U.S.A.
Mr. N. Halfweeg who was of great assistance in providing material, drawings and photographs from the Wijsmuller records.
Captain D. Hancox who selected salvage incidents and drawings which were of particular interest to me.

Stanford Maritime Limited
Member Company of the George Philip Group
12–14 Long Acre London WC2E 9LP
Editor D NICOLSON

First published 1979
© 1979 C N T Baptist

Printed in Great Britain by
Butler & Tanner Ltd, Frome and London

ISBN 0 540 07378 4

Contents

Introduction

In embarking on this book, I did so with the full realisation that I had limited expertise in this field and would have to rely heavily on others for material and advice. My justification, if one is necessary, must rest on my involvement with salvage work from time to time over a period of thirty-five years, during which time I have been privileged to share in some exciting salvage operations and have made a lot of friends in the industry.

I would like to dedicate this book to these fine people who repeatedly take their lives in their hands and whose skills and knowledge form the broad base on which the business continues to flourish. In doing this I would not like to omit those responsible for the technical advances, without which the salvage operator would be limited, and many a successful salvage operation would have had to be abandoned.

The main purpose of the book is to provide the reader with accounts of several salvage operations, highlighting different salvage problems, techniques and skills.

The success or failure of the individual operation has to be taken against the background of the difficulties involved in that particular job. Marine salvage is a high risk business in which only a few hard core Companies survive for any length of time. Salvage is not, and perhaps never has been, the get rich dream that many believe it to be. Unquestionably the lucky few have been in the right place at the right time and, with relatively little risk and effort, have profited beyond their normal expectations. This is unusual, and against the normal course of events.

In a highly competitive business, chance and luck play only a small part over the years. What really counts is good communication, organisation and equipment, combined with the necessary judgement and skills, so that the right tools are used on the right job with minimum risk to both men and equipment.

1 The principle of marine salvage

The principle of marine salvage is based on the concept that when a person or persons save or help to save a ship and/or her cargo from danger, in which the vessel and cargo could be badly damaged or lost, then the successful salvor is entitled to a reward. The successful salvor must not be the Master or a crew member of the endangered vessel, nor must he have in any way contributed to the circumstances which put the vessel in danger.

The legal basis to salvage

The British Merchant Shipping Act of 1894 and later amendments, deals with the whole question of marine salvage and covers salvage operations which take place in waters under British jurisdiction. British Courts of Admiralty handle salvage claims and the rewards for salvage service. Other major maritime nations normally have similar laws covering salvage operations in waters under their jurisdiction, and recognise the principle of salvage. It is important to remember though that there are exceptions.

Under the Maritime Conventions Act of 1911, the Master or person in charge of any British vessel shall, as far as he is able, and without serious danger to his own vessel and crew, render assistance to every person who is found at sea and is in danger of being lost, even if the person concerned is a subject of a foreign state at war with Great Britain. This Act is the instrument by which the British authorities gave recognition to International Maritime Agreements concerning 'life salvage'. It is important in as much as the saving of life at sea is placed outside the context of salvage by the Act. Saving life at sea becomes a duty and does not in itself constitute grounds for a salvage award.

Salvage is unique to the world of maritime affairs, and has no counterpart ashore. To earn a salvage award the salvor has to be successful and save the ship and/or her cargo. The degree to which he is successful will determine the amount of the salvage award, and the extent of damage to ship and cargo has to be taken into account. A ship may remain afloat and be towed into port in such

ORIGINAL

LLOYD'S

STANDARD FORM OF

SALVAGE AGREEMENT

(APPROVED AND PUBLISHED BY THE COMMITTEE OF LLOYD'S)

NO CURE—NO PAY

On board the Elwood Mead
Dated   Dec. 29   19 73

† It IS HEREBY AGREED between Captain.† Robert Noworyta
behalf of the Owners of the " M.V. Elwood Mead   " her cargo and
freight and Nan. G. Halfweeg   ", for and on behalf of B.V. Bureau Wijsmuller
(hereinafter called " the Contractor "):—

1. The Contractor agrees to use his best endeavours to salve the Elwood Mead
and/or her cargo and take them into   Rotterdam   or other
place to be hereafter agreed.   The services shall be rendered and accepted as
salvage services upon the principle of " no cure—no pay ". In case of arbitration being

† See Note 1
above

* See Note 2
above

NOTES.

1. Insert name of person signing on behalf of owners of property to be salved. The Master should sign wherever possible.

2. The Contractor's name should always be inserted in line 3 and wherever the Agreement is signed by the Master of the Salving vessel or other person on behalf of the Contractor the name of the Master or other person must also be inserted in the line 3 before the words " for and on behalf of". The words " for and on behalf of" should not be deleted where a Contractor signs personally.

for and on

Copy of an extract from the original agreement of a well-known salvage job.

poor condition that she is deemed to be a C.T.L. (Constructive Total Loss). Her value is therefore very much reduced and the award will take this into account. Damaged cargo is treated in the same way.

The important thing to remember is that the ship or cargo has to be worth salving. Nobody is under any obligation to take on a salvage operation. Those that do, have the option to:

i)   Set the terms of the contract in proportion to the services rendered under which they receive no salvage award, but payment as agreed under the terms of the contract.

ii) Agree salvage on a basis of 'No Cure, No Pay'. In this context Lloyd's Open Form is commonly used. The salvor or salvors are only paid if they are successful, and the amount will be awarded on the basis of the risk, time taken, equipment used and expense incurred as well as the value of the vessel and cargo salvaged after all the facts have been made available to the Legal Arbitrator.

Obviously when a vessel is disabled and a tug is taken under contract to find and tow her to a safe port, the terms of hire are likely to be a lot higher than a normal towage job involving the same distance if the vessel were being towed to the breakers yard.

The term 'salvage' in a broader context

The term 'salvage' or 'salvage operation' has, by common usage over the years, been corrupted beyond the legal definition, and has come to be used in a much broader framework where a salvage award may not necessarily be involved.

The lifting of sunken ships for the scrap value of the steel is an example. In the case of the German High Seas Fleet of World War I vintage, we have an example of a massive salvage operation which took place at Scapa Flow and involved a large number of vessels and a lifting operation that lasted several years. In this case no salvage award was involved. The sunken ships salvaged were classed as wrecks and therefore the property of the Crown. The would-be salvor had to obtain the permission of the British Admiralty and had to purchase the wrecks for a nominal sum.

Another type of salvage operation is the recovery of cargo from sunken ships – in particular valuable metals which are not adversely affected by prolonged immersion in salt water. In all such cases the recovered cargo, if landed in the U.K., must be reported to the Receiver of Wrecks for disposal. Depending on the age of the wreck and possible ownership of the cargo, the proceeds of the sale of such a cargo could be the subject of conflict in the courts. For this reason it is normal for the problem of ownership and the economic return for the salvor to be worked out as far as possible, well in advance.

The recovery of bullion from the strong rooms of sunken liners and treasure from ancient ships trading for the Phoenicians or the Spanish Treasure Fleet, have been the subject of much publicity. In most cases involving bullion, the appreciation of the precious metal over a period of years is likely to ensure that the salvors are adequately rewarded for their efforts, but again it is normal to ascertain the ownership of the cargo in question and, if the wreck is outside territorial limits, to ensure that it is landed in a country which will honour the salvors' efforts in accordance with any agreements which might have been signed, or with the customary generosity that the risk and effort involved, deserves.

In the case of sunken treasure from ancient ships wrecked inside territorial waters, the law varies from country to country. In most cases the State claims ownership, and permission to search for and recover such treasure may have to be obtained in advance. The would-be salvor could be in trouble with the law unless the necessary precautions are taken and agreements reached.

In recent years other types of specialised salvage operations have been undertaken by military and commercial salvage companies, these operations having involved a variety of tasks such as:

i)   The location and recovery of parts of a crashed aircraft from the seabed.
ii)   The location and recovery of nuclear weapons and midget submarines.
iii) The underwater excavation and recovery of ancient ships with no commercial value, but tremendous historical significance.

Salvage Tools

The tug

The tug is undoubtedly the tool most frequently used in salvage work. The assistance it can provide will vary considerably with the circumstances. Apart from towage to a safe port, the modern salvage tug is equipped with considerable potential to assist in fire fighting. Some have very large pumps capable of assisting in flooding compartments to correct a list, or pumping out others to increase buoyancy. Many have crew members on board who are experienced divers and can carry out underwater inspections and do limited simple repair jobs. The modern salvage tug is a versatile piece of equipment, not the least of its capabilities being a powerful radio station with which it can keep in touch with the distressed ship and summon specialised or additional help if necessary. Its primary use of course, is to tow vessels which are still afloat, or to help refloat vessels which may have gone aground.

The diver

Once a vessel has sunk or stranded with major damage, the tug on its own or with others to help it, are of little use, and the operation requires special equipment. In most cases the vessel will require the assistance of divers and sometimes a salvage ship. Often the work involved is heavily dependent on the effectiveness of the diver or diving team and the use of special equipment.

The salvage diver, other than those used aboard salvage tugs, is backed up by a considerable amount of special equipment for underwater work. Under water the diver becomes a multi-skilled craftsman capable of burning and welding, placing slings and directing lifting cranes or grabs, as the case may require. Yet he remains part of a team directed to fulfil a common purpose, which is the completion of the job in hand. A diver is extremely limited by his underwater environment. In many cases he can see very little – sometimes nothing at all, which compels him to work by feel or with artificial lighting aids.

In clear water and bright sunlight his vision is reduced and distorted. His isolation is complete without the safety line or telephone. As he immerses his body he is subjected to water pressure of 0.44 lb. per square inch for every foot of depth. True, he has a choice of diving equipment. Over the years, various types of equipment have been involved to allow him to work longer and to go to depths in excess of 1,000 feet. Diving in depths of up to 50 feet does not involve any special equipment or abnormal risk. Whether the diver uses a hard hat or helmet and suit combined with air hose, and air supplied from the surface, or a neoprene wet suit combined with air bottles, will depend largely on water temperature, visibility and the type of work to be undertaken. Inspections performed in depths of under 50 feet and involving less than one hour on the bottom do not normally require stops on the way up for decompression, or the use of a decompression chamber.

At greater depths the restraints placed on the diver are increased the deeper he goes. The air he breathes is compressed and he needs more of it to sustain life and work. His time on the bottom is reduced by depth increases, and he has to spend proportionately longer on decompression on the way up. During the last ten to fifteen years the use of mixed gas (oxygen and helium) for breathing, has increased the diver's capability to go deeper, without the restrictions of armoured suits fitted with articulated joints and designed to resist pressure at great depths.

Saturation diving techniques are expensive and involve the use of special pressurised chambers on the surface in which a number of divers can live under controlled conditions for extended periods. The theory is that after a given period under part pressure, a diver's body becomes saturated with inert gas and he can live and dive for extended periods without absorbing more. Living under pressure and utilising diving bells connected by special air locks to the living quarters, divers transfer in safety and can work for extended periods at depths between 300 and 1500 feet without decompression or suffering any harm.

Saturation diving requires heavy expenditure and is only used for major underwater operations requiring a group of divers to work for prolonged periods in deep water. Up to the present time, it is not in general use in salvage work, and tends to be restricted commercially to offshore oilfield operations and associated work.

The salvage ship

The salvage ship comes in many shapes and sizes and needs to be small enough to be manoeuvrable, yet large enough to carry a great deal of special equipment and the men to use it. It must be of shallow draft, able to approach larger vessels which have run aground, without herself grounding or sustaining damage. In the case of sunken wrecks she must be equipped to search and find them without losing too much time, and then lay moorings around the sunken vessel so she can moor over it. Once in position she becomes a work platform for divers and equipment of various kinds, depending on the particular operation. Sometimes she may have to lift heavy weights or provide power and air. Each operation is unique and requires different equipment and techniques.

When used in the open sea and areas where bad weather can be the rule rather than the exception, seaworthiness is a major requirement. The ability to vacate moorings, secure equipment quickly and safely, and to withstand the batterings of major gales, is essential.

2 The salvage company

As far as it can be determined, the professional salvage company is associated with the evolvement of the tug, or more precisely the deep sea tug. The British firm of Watkins was the first company to enter this field, and since then many others have sprung up all over the world. Today the Dutch companies, represented by Smit & Co. based at Rotterdam and the Bureau Wijsmuller based at Ijmuiden, are front runners in an international field where competition is fierce and many have failed to survive the tests of time.

What are the ingredients for success in the salvage business? To answer this question one must really examine the potential for doing business.

First of all, to obtain salvage work you need a ship or ships in difficulties which require the services of a professional salvor. Shipowners and masters of big expensive ships are the last people to willingly get into this type of trouble, so salvage jobs are a matter of luck. Bad luck for the owner, master and crew of the ship concerned; good luck for the professional salvor. It is unfortunately a fact of life that salvage is only made possible as the direct result of the misfortunes of others. Apart from the normal marine casualties resulting from collision, stranding and fire, the most profitable hunting grounds for a would-be salvor are disaster areas. These might be a port or coast which has been swept by tropical storm or, more generally, narrow navigational highways such as the English Channel, with its high traffic density and weather conditions varying from calms and dense fog through a fairly broad spectrum, to severe gales and storms.

Salvage companies frequently come into being to perform special functions outside the scope of the normal salvage award. Such outfits may clear a harbour of wrecks, remove dangerous goods from a sunken ship, or bullion from an ocean liner. Once the specific job is done, the salvage crew are paid off, the equipment sold and the company liquidated. To survive and prosper over the long term, the professional salvage company needs other work, or its running costs will be unbearable and ultimately result in bankruptcy.

Normally, a large salvage company will try to provide a harbour tug service at its home port and sometimes even contract tugs to provide such services at other ports. Ocean towage is another area which provides a regular income. Through brokers all over the world the salvage company management can find out what towage jobs are available.

Old ships are frequently bought in one location and towed half way around the world to the breakers' yard. Dredgers and barges frequently have to be moved long distances by sea. Another profitable source of income is the ocean towage of drilling rigs and pipe-laying barges.

Through the routine, or bread and butter service it provides, the salvage company builds its reputation for ability to perform and the dependability of its equipment and ships. A reputation for dependability and good equipment, coupled with a sound financial background, is a necessity for the successful operator. If any of these ingredients are missing, the word soon gets around and important contracts are given to competitors.

Today, salvage is the jam on the everyday bread and butter business of a towage and salvage company. To remain healthy the company has to tread a financial tight rope, replacing old tugs with new and maintaining a staff of technical experts and equipment in reserve against the sudden requirements of a big salvage job. The Bureau Wijsmuller is a typical salvage company which has stood the test of time. The Company was founded by Johannes Franciscus Wijsmuller, who was born in Amsterdam in 1877. His career has already been recorded in great detail, and it is sufficient for our purposes to acknowledge that he not only pioneered the delivery of new vessels by unconventional means, but founded the existing Company just prior to World War I with his tug called the *Holland*, a coal burner of 500 h.p. Within ten years he had a total of nineteen ocean going tugs, twenty-six sea-going and harbour tugs, as well as a number of cargo ships.

The Bureau's main office was located at The Hague until 1921 when it was moved to Rotterdam. Johannes Franciscus Wijsmuller died in 1923 and it was not until 1930 that the Company moved to Ijmuiden, where it is still located. After the death of the founder, the Company fell on hard times, none of his children being old enough to take an active part. Effective control passed out of the hands of the Wijsmuller family, and it was not until after World War II that the second generation of Wijsmullers became active in the marine business of delivering ships, and also in the

Wijsmuller Navigation Company Inc., a shipping agency located in New York and founded by John F. Wijsmuller.

In 1955, at the invitation of the Goedkoop family, who had a controlling interest in Bureau Wijsmuller, J. F. Wijsmuller took over the management of the Bureau Wijsmuller, and commenced rebuilding the Company. In 1957 Arthur Wijsmuller became manager, and by 5th September 1961 Bureau Wijsmuller came back under family control, and Arthur Wijsmuller became the managing director.

In 1968, by mutual agreement, the five Wijsmuller brothers decided to separate their various business interests, with the result that the Company came under the sole control of Arthur Wijsmuller.

Under John F. Wijsmuller, the Company commenced a period of recovery and expansion which was consolidated by Arthur Wijsmuller. From a technical standpoint, when John F. Wijsmuller took over the direction of Bureau Wijsmuller, the tug fleet consisted of:

> *Noord Holland* – 2600 h.p.
> *Cycloop* – 1200 h.p.
> *Hector, Stentor, Nestor* – three old tugs, each with limited power, 600 h.p.

Two new tugs, the *Titan* and *Friesland*, sister ships to the *Cycloop*, were under construction. The *Noord Holland* was the only tug in the fleet with an engine rated over 2000 h.p., which at the time was deemed by many to be the lower limit practical for heavy towing work across the oceans of the world.

To make sure the Company was in a position to compete on an international basis, John Wijsmuller, through his American connections, acquired two more American tugs each with a rated h.p. of about 2500. They were named the *Zeeland* and *Utrecht*, and were destined to perform many profitable tows. The old tugs were scrapped and gradually replaced by the *Cycloop* class, though each successive vessel was an improvement on the original.

In many ways the *Cycloop* represented the ideal compromise in size and economy. The limited size made it highly suitable for harbour work at Ijmuiden, yet these vessels were powerful enough and capable of undertaking towage and salvage jobs all over the world. Their excellent design and low speed diesels made them manoeuvrable and economic units.

Arthur Wijsmuller is perhaps best remembered for his good

sense and sound business judgement. He continued to expand the Company, treading a careful path which catered for the growing need for more and bigger tugs, without overstretching financially. The loss of the *Noord Holland* which was confiscated by the Indonesian government was a serious blow, but in 1963 two new tugs of approximately 3000 h.p. were added to the fleet. They were named the *Groningen* and *Gelderland*. The following year *Willem Barendz* and *Jacob van Heemskerch*, each of 5375 h.p. joined the fleet.

Apart from tugs, Arthur Wijsmuller could see the potential of special salvage vessels. He acquired two old boom defence vessels and renamed them *Help* and *Octopus*. In addition to salvage work, these vessels were used for maintenance work on oil sealine terminals and wreck removal. In 1969 the new salvage vessel *Krab* replaced the two older ships.

The Bureau Wijsmuller fleet continued to undergo changes. Older vessels were sold or up-graded by extensive engine modifications which resulted in considerable power increases, but competition was fierce and the need was for newer and more powerful tugs to handle the requirements of V.L.C.C.'s (Very Large Crude Oil Carriers), and the enormous drilling rigs which were coming into service. Arthur Wijsmuller spent much of his time travelling, keeping contact with his clients all over the world, and selling the Wijsmuller know-how and expertise.

As well as a fine towage and salvage fleet, a strong organisation ashore was built up. On the top floor of their offices at Ijmuiden, a radio room was constructed which permitted round the clock listening watch on all the major distress frequencies, and permitted Wijsmuller tugs all over the world to keep head office informed of likely jobs or problems. A technical staff of salvage and shipping experts were on call 24 hours a day to fly anywhere in the world, and a considerable quantity of salvage equipment was available at Ijmuiden to be flown out to the assistance of any ship that needed it.

Salvage is not only a practical matter, but is resolved through arbitration or in the courts. It was not an accident that Dr. J. Frank Wijsmuller should qualify in the legal profession, and on the death of his father Arthur Wijsmuller in 1973, took over the control of Bureau Wijsmuller.

Frank Wijsmuller had all the advantages of a modern business and legal education, which were brought to bear on the streamlining and rationalising of the organisation while still continuing a policy of upgrading the fleet with modern and more powerful tugs.

The tug *Amsterdam* with her fully automated engine room and an indicated h.p. of 7500 was bought in 1974, and two even more powerful tugs were ordered in the same year.

The Bureau Wijsmuller has been fortunate in the quality of its crews. Many European firms, including Dutch companies, have been unable to get sufficient men to go to sea to retain the same nationality at all levels. The type of work, good wages and the chance of salvage have been factors which have worked in the Company's favour. Air conditioning and improved living accommodation has also been a big incentive to keeping good crews contented. High morale is essential where the crews of salvage ships and tugs are concerned. This, coupled with opportunities for advancement in an expanding fleet, keep the right blend of experience and youth together, so that Bureau Wijsmuller represents a career job with above average rewards in terms of excitement and hard cash.

In terms of skills, the crews of salvage ships and tugs have to be above average. Seamanship is a must at all levels and the master has to be able to manoeuvre his vessel to connect up heavy towing gear in rough weather. The mate and seamen must be capable of working on a pitching deck and controlling heavy wires and shackles without killing each other. Many of the younger seamen are trained progressively first to tend divers, then to dive and use underwater cutting and welding gear. For these services they are paid extra.

The engine room staff have to be sound marine engineers, resourceful in getting salvage pumps and other machinery such as compressors working, in the most difficult circumstances, and sometimes under conditions which involve a great deal of personal risk.

Salvage work in modern times frequently requires more than sound seamanship and the courage to undertake dangerous work. Frequently, special knowledge is required which only a naval architect can supply. Other specialist knowledge, such as the handling of dangerous goods, may also be necessary. More and more salvage work requires a team effort ashore and afloat. The commercial and legal risks have to be weighed and covered, and the would-be client legally committed to signing Lloyd's Open Form, or some other document which formally commits him to pay for the service he obtains. A vessel such as an oil tanker can be salvaged, but in a damaged condition it may be difficult to get permission to allow her to enter a port, particularly if there is any risk of oil pollution.

The Company's salvage inspector plays an important roll. To some extent he is the bridge between the home organisation that controls and plans each major salvage operation, and the work force that actually does the job. He may control and coordinate the activities of several vessels and a large salvage team, but perhaps his biggest responsibility is to use his experience and judgement so that money and effort are not wasted in hopeless efforts.

Lloyd's Open Form – 'No Cure, No Pay' – means exactly what it says, and there is little point in spending time and money on hopeless salvage cases, or those where the vessel is so badly damaged that the cost of salvaging her exceeds the worth of the vessel.

3   Wartime salvage tug

The destructive forces involved in war provide ample scope for marine salvage when such hostilities are extended to embrace the marine environment. The British Admiralty and the American Navy had fairly large organisations and a variety of salvage ships and tugs to cover their needs all over the world.

In the case of the British Admiralty, some of these vessels were under the White Ensign and had naval crews, mainly drawn from the Naval Reserve, but having experience in the type of vessels in which they sailed. Others remained under the Red Ensign, and though controlled by the Admiralty, operated in theory at least as normal commercial vessels.

The British Admiralty classed all tugs under their control in three main categories:

A Class tugs – defined as ocean going salvage tugs which could proceed in the heaviest North Atlantic weather.

B Class tugs – defined as salvage tugs which could also be used for assisting ships in harbour, and which could proceed in all but the heaviest North Atlantic weather.

C Class tugs – suitable for harbour work and work in the estuaries of large rivers, but which would not normally go more than 200 miles from land.

The above broad definitions may not be exact, but they serve to show the way the Admiralty classified a variety of civilian craft, many of which fled from occupied Europe.

The A Class tug *Salvonia* belonged to the Overseas Towage and Salvage Company. It was a large oil burning steam tug with remarkably graceful lines, and though built prior to the war had the high flaring bows that are the true hall-mark of the ocean going tug. The following incidents were narrated by her second mate.

The *Salvonia* left Milford Haven in gale conditions, as part of a small convoy bound up the Irish Sea, planning to join up with a larger convoy in the North Channel, then to proceed round the

'Emerald Isle' before heading south for Gibraltar. The *Salvonia* acted as rescue ship for an escort carrier for the early part of the voyage, but in due course broke off and proceeded, at her best speed of about 12 knots, independently to Horta, Fayal Island, in the Azores.

At the time in question, Britain had taken advantage of an old treaty with Portugal to establish a small Naval base at Horta. When the *Salvonia* arrived, Naval Headquarters were located in a badly damaged frigate which had had her stern blown off, but was otherwise intact. She had been towed in and moored securely alongside the breakwater, and housed the Senior British Naval Officer and his staff. The S.B.N.O. Horta, as he was called, had a small fleet of ships under his control. Most of the Naval vessels were trawlers armed with a single 4-inch gun and depth charges for use against submarines.

These vessels were mainly coal burners and were crewed by Naval Reserve personnel. A large oiler was moored in the centre of Horta Harbour, and vessels which required fuel oil went alongside to bunker. In addition, there was another tug, smaller and with less horsepower, but under the White Ensign. Her name was *Empire Sampson*.

The main importance of Horta at that time, was as a fuelling station for small vessels bound from America to the United Kingdom. At a later stage this included whole fleets of Naval and merchant vessels which were to be used for the Normandy invasion. The level of activity was fairly low; the Naval trawlers did an anti-submarine patrol off Horta and also at Lagens Bay where an airfield was under construction.

The *Salvonia's* main occupation was to lie at her moorings while the crew chipped and painted her or overhauled the massive cable-laid hawsers used for long distance towing. She had one 18-inch-diameter hawser and two 12-inch hawsers, together with an assortment of large wires. The hawsers were manilla ropes, and for some reason the rats loved to eat the strands in odd places.

By modern standards she was very limited in terms of horsepower and manoeuvrability, and as she was not equipped with a towing winch, the heavy hawsers and wires had to be rigged by hand and used in conjunction with a massive towing hook. Her reciprocating engine was reliable but she was fitted with low pressure Scotch boilers which consumed large quantities of fuel when steaming at full speed, and limited her range and endurance. By comparison with modern ocean going tugs, she left much to be desired in every respect, but for all that she was a fine little vessel, and in capable hands could perform wonderfully when other and more powerful tugs failed.

Her second mate recalled how they were sent off to sea in a hurry one night, and steamed off towards Newfoundland to rendezvous with a small British merchant vessel that had taken a Flower class corvette in tow. The wartime need for radio silence made such a rendezvous with other vessels a chancy business and, on arriving at the given position, *Salvonia* found nothing. After searching ten miles either side of the course, their quarry was reported to be steering towards the rendezvous. Settling down to conserve fuel, they waited for her in steadily deteriorating weather conditions, steaming in what could best be described as a circle, using a zig zag course and reduced speed to confuse any enemy submarines which might sight them.

Twenty four hours after the scheduled rendezvous was due to have occurred, the master gave up and decided to head back for Horta at an economic speed, in what was by then a force 10 gale. The gale had produced a large swell that ran towards the north east and their course was at right angles to it, with the effect that they were continuously climbing up a watery mountain slope, rolling or spilling over the top and careering rapidly down the far side in a flurry of spume and spindrift. Despite such conditions, her huge screw and the steady even thrust of her engine steadied her, and they were well able to appreciate her sea keeping qualities when they fell in with a modern diesel-electric tug flying the U.S. flag, closing with them on a converging course.

A little later they received a radio message giving them a new rendezvous. Increasing to full speed and leaving their American friends they altered course for the southern tip of Flores to try to take over the corvette they had been looking for. The merchant vessel was having trouble in the heavy swell. In due course they caught up with her and the transfer was effected with some difficulty.

The corvette was a comparatively small vessel, so they used a 12-inch hawser, all 120 fathoms of it, together with 60 fathoms of $3\frac{1}{2}$-inch wire. The hawser once rigged, had to be fitted with chafing leathers in way of the chafing bars, which in turn were greased to provide a minimum of friction. The time it took to tow the vessel to the anchorage at Horta was relatively short, and seemed hardly to justify the use of such heavy gear, and the soaking they received rigging it.

It was the first time the second mate had experienced the horrors of shortening the tow line as they came into the anchorage. Old tug hands are perhaps the only people who know what a difficult and dangerous job this can be in a rough sea, with only the main deck capstan and a messenger rope for help. The hawsers were too big to take around the capstan, so a messenger rope had to be used in conjunction with a snatch block located as far forward as possible. The towing hawser was hauled in, in bights, and stoppered off each time sufficient was recovered. The wet rope had to be kept slack all the time, and this was done by the mate signalling the master, who was using his engines to help.

On this particular occasion they recovered the entire hawser as fast as they could, and used the wire pennant to tow the little warship to a suitable anchorage, where it awaited divers who could cut away the wire rope that had inadvertently got around her screw.

On anchoring their tow, the mate and second mate got orders to clear the maindeck as quickly as possible. Busy with the towing gear, they had not noticed the Naval signalman on the bridge working the signal lamp, and it appeared they had a second job in quick succession.

Rounding the breakwater they saw a 6-inch gun cruiser, the H.M.S. *Glasgow* aground just ahead of the oiler. Presumably she had entered the harbour, gone alongside the oiler and bunkered, perhaps taken a bit more oil than was prudent, and gone aground whilst leaving.

Amid a flurry of signals, orders and counter orders from the bridge of the cruiser, they moved to her assistance, to find the large U.S. tug they had left earlier, already pulling at full power, and the *Empire Sampson* pushing from the other side. The American tug had a flurry of foam under her stern, and the wire stretched taut from her towing winch to a set of bits on the cruiser's quarter deck.

'He hasn't got enough room to use his power properly,' commented the *Salvonia*'s skipper. Sure enough, nothing happened. As if the gold bedecked Captain on the cruiser's bridge had read his mind, a stream of orders from the cruiser's bridge resulted in the American tug letting go, and the *Salvonia* being ordered to take her place. The second mate suspected the Captain's decision was based on racial prejudice rather than a comparison of the power of the two tugs. Perhaps the Captain of the *Glasgow* knew about professional salvage tugs, and their skippers!

The problem of towing H.M.S. *Glasgow* off would have been

a simple one had there been more room between the cruiser's starboard side and the breakwater. What was needed was a strong thrust to move the vessel's stern sideways towards the breakwater, and at the same time move her stern off the shallow spit which extended out from shore with a tapered finger pointing at the breakwater.

One solution would have been to push from the port side of the cruiser, but the tanker's anchor and shallow water made it difficult even for the *Empire Sampson*, while on the starboard side of the cruiser there was hardly room for the *Salvonia* to swing at right angles between the cruiser's starboard side and the breakwater. They went alongside and took a wire from her. The skipper insisted on rather more slack than the Navy wanted to give them, but when he was satisfied the eye of the wire was put on the towing hook ready for a supreme effort.

Keeping the towing wire slack, the skipper ordered a manilla spring run from the starboard bow to the breakwater, and used this in conjunction with an ahead engine movement to swing the tug's bows away from the cruiser, and towards the breakwater.

As all this preparation was done in an unhurried manner, with the limited manpower available, it provoked a great deal of impatience on the cruiser's bridge. When the *Salvonia* was pointing about 60 degrees from the cruiser, the master ordered 'Helm amidship', and 'Let go spring', followed by 'Full Ahead'. The tug jerked forward, and the wire twanged taut, arresting the tug's forward movement with only feet between her bows and the breakwater.

The jerk, with the full weight of the tug on it had been enough. The cruiser's stern came clear and the water under her counter boiled as she headed for open water, towing her rescuer broadside at an ever-increasing angle.

Dimly, the second mate was aware of the skipper yelling at the mate to trip the towing hook, and shouts from the main deck that the tow wire was hard against the port stop and the hook was jammed. In the split seconds before disaster, somebody on the cruiser let the wire go from the other end, and they were back on an even keel and none the worse for the experience.

It took a little while to restore collective dignities, and the incident did nothing to enhance the Navy's standing with those on board. The technique used to dislodge the grounded cruiser was never discussed or remarked on but, for all that, it was a perfect illustration of knowing how to use the tug's weight to impose a shock load at the correct angle to get results when towing power alone failed.

During the time *Salvonia* spent in the Azores, a large variety of salvage jobs were undertaken, some of them successful, others doomed to failure. She operated as far south as the African coast, and north to the Grand Banks of Newfoundland.

On one occasion they were sent to assist a torpedoed aircraft carrier in a U.S. task force, not far from the Canary Islands, and another time to a sinking ship, half way between Iceland and the Azores. In both cases they were disappointed, and were recalled because the vessels had either sunk, or someone else got there first. It was frustrating never to know what had happened.

Some very successful work was done towards the end of their stay in the Azores as a result of assistance provided by the U.S. Air Force which was operating out of Lagens Airfield on the Island Terracia. An aircraft was used to find the crippled ship and report back, giving a position and course to steer by signal lamp. One particular 'flying fortress' was either lucky or very skilled at that type of work.

The longest tow they made was a merchant ship called the *City of Omaha*. She was an old cargo ship registered in New Orleans, and flying the U.S. flag. This vessel lost her rudder several hundred miles east of Cape Race, and they found her and her escort with the assistance of their airborne friends. The master wanted to go to Falmouth, and requested the *Salvonia* to connect up aft to steer him whilst he used his own engines.

The skipper of the *Salvonia* had different ideas and refused point blank to any plans which involved acting as a floating rudder, on the grounds that this never was a practical solution for long distances in rough weather. Finally the master of the disabled ship gave in and disconnected his starboard anchor from the chain. A messenger was hove on board through a panama lead, and eventually the big $5\frac{1}{2}$-inch diameter wire was shackled to the anchor chain. The wire was paid out and, as the *Salvonia* moved away, all 120 fathoms of the big 18-inch towing hawser. When this was all out, the ship paid out 180 feet of chain while moving slowly ahead. With the required amount of chain out, the windlass brake was applied, and the chain secured by additional wire lashings to make sure that more chain did not run out whilst towing.

On board the *Salvonia*, the chafing bars were greased and heavy duty leathers secured to the large hawser in the areas where chafe was likely to occur. Everything was ready and the long tow started as they gradually worked up to full speed. The rudderless ship yawed badly from one side to another, but never badly enough to cause the weighted tow line to come out of the water or to seriously affect their course and speed.

For most of the trip they experienced a following wind and sea without any dangerously bad weather, averaging over 8 knots throughout the trip, and there were no problems with the towing gear. It is interesting to note that the *City of Omaha* tried using her engines from time to time, but this only caused her to increase the yaw, and did little to increase speed.

Off the Lizard and while still in relatively deep water, they stopped towing, and the *City of Omaha* hove in all the anchor chain till the shackle connecting the chain to the wire was inboard. They then continued till harbour tugs came out to meet them outside Falmouth, when they stopped and the ship let the towing wire go, leaving them to the tedious job of recovering the hawser and wire.

The salvage jobs described were not spectacular or exciting, but most ordinary salvage jobs which involve a tug connecting up her tow line are unromantic and plain hard work. Occasionally salvage means real danger and a lot of excitement, though this does not always involve the rescue of a big ship or large salvage awards.

One such incident happened a couple of days after the *Salvonia* had successfully towed the *City of Omaha* to Falmouth. They were bound north for the Clyde and the repair yard, when orders were received to proceed to the rescue of a small Naval auxiliary which was in distress off the north Cornish coast. They had difficulty locating the little vessel, and were finally directed to her by a Canadian frigate. She turned out to be a little drift net fisherman, requisitioned for the duration of hostilities.

The tiny vessel had suffered an engine breakdown with complete power failure. Adrift in a rough sea, she had been carried by current and tide right under the cliffs, and had let go her anchor to try to save herself. Unfortunately, the anchor and chain had carried away and she had drifted even closer to the grim line of the breakers at the base of the cliff before her spare anchor caught and stopped her drifting to certain destruction.

The question was whether the skipper of the *Salvonia* could get near enough to pass a line without endangering his own ship and crew. There was no time to evaluate all the angles, as the drifter was riding to a single wire. Should it part or the anchor drag, they would be smashed on the rocks in seconds.

Telling the mate to get the line throwing gun ready, and with the second mate at the wheel, the skipper backed the *Salvonia* down to leeward, and towards the little fishing vessel. Keeping the tug's head into the sea, he used ahead movements and port rudder to straighten her up when she broached, working the engine gently astern, and allowing the wind and sea to help move the tug towards the shore.

The towering cliffs looked formidable and ominously close. The second mate could not see where he was going as his station at the wheel prevented a good look, and the big funnel blocked his view aft. It seemed that the cliffs reached out on either side, looming right over them.

The whole operation took about ninety minutes of which they spent thirty minutes going astern towards the drifter. At the time it seemed they had been moving astern for half a lifetime. The crack of the line-throwing gun and excited cries from the deck told the second mate they were there. It was a relief to hear the mate shout 'He's got our line on board', and after a pause: 'It's all fast!'

Now they began to move ahead, slowly paying out the tow line until they were back in deep water. Then, as the weight came on the towing gear the skipper ordered the signalman to tell the tow to slip his anchor, and they began to pull her clear and out of danger.

They towed the little Naval drifter to Dale Roads in Milford Haven, and it wasn't till the big signal light on Saint Anne's Head asked the *Salvonia* why their tow's ensign was at half mast, that they became aware that some of the little ship's crew had been killed in the engine room.

4 The lame duck to the rescue

Salvage is frequently unexpected and can take place in the most unusual circumstances. The following incident was related by the first mate of the *Esso Cadillac*.

In the late 1940's I was first mate of an 11,000 d.w.t. (deadweight tons) tanker called the *Esso Cadillac* belonging to Esso Petroleum Co. Ltd. and registered in London. An old motor ship with a single auxiliary Scotch boiler and capable of a maximum speed of 11 knots, she was built on the Tyne, and was originally called the *Empire Bronze* rechristened later by E.P.Co. when they bought her after the war.

On this occasion we were bound from Aruba in the Dutch West Indies to Hull with several grades of clean oil, such as aviation gasoline, motor spirit and kerosene. The trip home had been unremarkable except for more than the usual number of engine stops at sea, largely due to the fact that we were overdue for dry dock and repairs, and were scheduled to go to a repair yard on the Tyne after discharging at Saltend, near Hull.

We had made our way up the Channel in good weather, but just before reaching Dungeness received orders to discharge part of our cargo at Purfleet on the Thames, always referred to by seafarers as the London River. On passing Dungeness we contacted the Trinity House pilot cutter, and in due course picked up our pilot.

At this point the trouble started. The chief engineer followed the pilot up the bridge ladder.

'I have an emergency in the engine room,' he declared. 'We must go to anchor as quickly as possible. All my feed pumps are broken down – I'll shortly have to shut the boiler off, and the ship will be dead in about thirty minutes.'

Without much discussion the master and pilot agreed that the best place to anchor was in the small bay just east of Dungeness, as this would put the ship out of the main shipping route and provide shelter from westerly gales.

In due course the little ship (by modern standards) came safely to anchor, and the 'Not Under Command' signal was hoisted so that passing ships would keep clear. Meanwhile, the engineers had shut off the boiler fires and allowed the boiler to start cooling down.

After making sure everything was secure forward, I was called to a meeting to discuss the emergency, in the master's day room. Perhaps 'discuss' is the wrong word, for the master was a fiery little Welshman who didn't believe in discussion groups. The Trinity House pilot, chief engineer and myself only answered questions when addressed directly, and I would hasten to add that none of us felt there was anything unusual in this procedure.

The chief explained that the ship was equipped with two steam feed pumps to put water into the boiler. One had broken down a few days before and was completely dismantled as the engineers were busy repairing it. The other pump had failed as a result of a fracture in the crosshead, which was probably caused by a flaw in the steel.

'How long will it take to repair?' asked the master.

'About twenty four hours. It means taking the crosshead off the other pump and replacing the broken one.'

'We will be able to proceed then by this time tomorrow morning?'

'No,' replied the chief. 'The feed pumps may be the least of our problems. In getting to anchor safely, I lost the water out of the boiler gauge glass and it will take us twelve hours to let the boiler cool down, and then we need to open it up and see if it is damaged. If it is damaged badly, we can't get steam up. If it is undamaged, we will then have to find some way to put 12–20 tons in the boiler, close it up and start to raise steam by hand.'

'You see,' he continued, 'This is a wartime built ship. We have no emergency diesel generator, and a lot of the pumps are attached pumps which are run off the main engine or driven by steam. You need the main engine running, or the boiler working to run any of the auxiliaries.'

'Does that mean we'll have no lights at night, chief?'

'That's right. My advice is to get the ship towed in. It may be impossible to get going again.'

Nobody spoke, and after a few minutes the master resumed. 'Chief, I want you to go back to the engine room and look at the situation once more, but this time positively. You are going to fix those pumps, and get steam up, and this ship will get underway *without* assistance! Discuss your manpower requirements with the second engineer, and work the engineers and other staff on twelve hour watches split down the centre, with the second responsible for the first twelve hours, and you the rest of the time. Lay out a schedule and let me know when the boiler is cool enough to inspect. If there is no damage, forget about filling it, the mate can handle that. Let him know what emergency lighting you want and additional manpower to assist in the engine room. I'm sending a message to the owners to tell them we are anchored for emergency repairs which will take an estimated forty eight hours.'

The meeting broke up. I went to call 'sparks' to tell him the captain wanted to send an urgent message to the owners, and then went about the business of getting ready for what I knew would be a major effort and endurance test.

It is doubtful in these days of V.H.F. and long distance radio telephones whether any master would want, or could have contained his problems to the ship. Today, the owners would possibly want to talk to the chief engineer direct on the phone, and might override the master's decision if they agreed with the chief engineer.

The ship was promptly organised to deal with the emergency. The second and third mates kept the anchor watch unassisted. The carpenter made ready all the navigation and emergency oil lights, and battery lamps were provided for messrooms and alleyways. Emergency lighting in the engine room consisted of battery operated work torches, supplemented by brilliant lighting obtained by connecting 12-volt batteries to Aldis lamp bulbs in the vicinity of the feed pumps. All personnel not engaged in repairing the feed pumps or other essential jobs went to their bunks to rest as soon as the evening meal had been served.

Just before midnight, the engineers had the boiler opened up and the chief and second engineer undertook an inspection to see if any damage had been sustained. After about an hour, both men were in agreement that no serious damage had been done. From that point on, the task of filling the boiler by hand began.

A small hose was fitted to the starboard after galley hand pump and two stewards, the second cook and a cabin boy took it in turns to work the hand pump, which sent a small jet of water into the open manhole on the boiler top. The rest of the crew formed a continuous chain gang which drew water out of the after peak with a bucket on the end of a heaving line, and passed it up the human chain until the water was dumped in the manhole at the top of the boiler. The empty buckets were passed back on a shorter chain without interrupting the flow of full buckets on their way to the top of the boiler.

Every ten minutes each man moved up and round one place in the chain and a new man took his turn hauling water from the after peak. In this way the men changed position and worked up the chain of full buckets, and then down the return chain handling empty buckets, till finally they arrived at the last position and had an hour off to relax and get a hot drink and a sandwich. The idea was to try to keep the water going into the boiler continuously. The master and I both took turns in the chain, but one of us always remained on deck in case of emergencies.

The galley pump worked well at first, but gradually the four willing stewards grew tired, and the amount of water put into the boiler grew steadily less. By 0330 the pump had broken down and the weary foursome were told to get some rest prior to helping the cook get breakfast.

The chain gang worked fairly well. At first the novelty kept everybody cheerful and jokes were made when water was spilt, or a bucket was dropped. As time went on the men became less talkative and carried on grimly. By 0500 everyone was weary and the master decided to call a halt at 0600 for an early breakfast and resume at 0800. By 0600 there was no sign of water in the gauge glass, but the second engineer felt that considerable progress had been made and that another six hours' work would give us more than half a gauge glass.

Work was resumed at 0800 and stopped again at noon, by which time there was less than an inch showing in the gauge glass. At 1400 hours work was resumed, and by 1530 the chief engineer considered that there was enough water in the boiler, and the chain gang was treated to a tot of rum.

While the boiler was being filled, the feed pump had been repaired, but it could not be tested. The engine room gang had plenty to do. The emergency hand fuel pump was checked over and preparations made to box up the boiler prior to putting a fire under it.

At 1700 the boiler was ready, and everyone was given a break for the evening meal. The emergency fuel pump was hand operated and four men were assigned to turn it, all four being changed after 20 minutes. Normally the pump could be operated by two strong men, but everyone was weary, and frequent relief was the only alternative.

The boiler was warmed through with a single fire, and everything seemed to take an eternity. By 0100 the next day the steam gauge started to register, and by 0300 we had enough steam to switch to the steam pumps for fuel and boiler water feed. After the feed pump had been checked out, the steam generator was started and the emergency lighting dispensed with. The chief engineer wanted time to check the boiler out and warm the engine through, so it was decided that everybody would have an early breakfast. Normal watches would be reset at 0800.

The *Esso Cadillac* got underway at 0830, and after seeing the anchors secured, I reported to the bridge.

'Our orders have been changed. We are going direct to Hull,' said our indomitable captain, as we nosed up Channel. 'Better get a shower and some rest, mate.' So we proceeded, with Folkestone abeam to port, and a freshening northerly wind sending spray over the foredeck.

It did not take me long to shower and climb into my bunk, and by 0930 I was asleep. At 1030 the third mate called me. 'You're wanted on the bridge, mate. We're going to the rescue of a small coaster.'

Dragging myself out of a deep sleep, which only the truly weary appreciate, I climbed into my clothes, and then in full appreciation of what I'd just heard, pulled on my sea boots and oilskins. On the bridge, I became aware that we were level with the Goodwin Sands, and the wind had freshened to a northerly gale which was whipping up a nasty cross sea.

'North Foreland radio has reported a coaster in distress,' stated the captain. 'Apparently it is the *Success* of London, with a crew of three. From what we can make out, she is about 7 miles ahead of us with her engine broken down, and anchored fairly close to a sandbank. I plan to get to windward of her and a little up tide, drop the anchor and allow the wind and tide to carry us as close as possible to her. The second mate will fire a line over her, and you must see that there is plenty of gear, small cordage and ropes, for the job before you go for'd to let go the anchors.'

With the maindeck awash it was no easy job to get a weary crew to transfer all the items from the rope locker to the poop. Fortunately, there were ample large manilla mooring ropes aft, and within thirty minutes I was able to inform the captain that everything was ready aft.

'Very well, Mr. Mate. I'm afraid you and the carpenter are going to get very wet for'd while you are tending the anchors. Hang on to something firm, and don't forget to let me know how the chain leads every few minutes. I'll use the starboard anchor and the usual hand signals, so watch me carefully.' Made oversize by my oilskins,

I felt the thrust of the gale as the carpenter and I made our way for'd and cleared the anchors ready for dropping. Every other wave sent a fairly solid curtain of spray over us, and the vessel's uneasy motion made our foothold precarious.

In due course, the ship reached the required position and the master gave the necessary hand signal. 'Chippy' was watching me closely, and as I relayed the signal from the bridge, he released the brake on the starboard anchor chain.

The next couple of hours were wet and miserable, and we could not see from for'd what was going on aft. Apparently, several attempts to fire rocket lines over the *Success* failed, and a messenger line was floated down to the vessel with the aid of two 40-gallon drums. Finally, the three men were able to heave the end of the heavy manilla tow rope on board and secure it. This was no small feat, as the little ship was without power of any kind.

With the tow line secure, the order was given to heave up the anchor, and we got underway once again, proceeding at slow speed to nurse the tow line and ease the strain on the tow which was attempting to help by using her manual steering equipment. It was decided to make for the Sunk Lightship in the south of the Thames, where the owners of the *Success* were requested to provide a tug to tow her to safety.

Communication with the tow was limited. The men on board did not appear to have a signal lamp or any other means of signalling. It was about this time a lifeboat arrived on the scene in answer to the original distress signal. She had put out from the Kent coast, and came alongside on the lee side. We asked the coxswain to take some food and cigarettes over to the crew of the *Success*. This the men of the Kentish lifeboat did willingly. However, when they got alongside, they found that the crew wanted to abandon the vessel, and were only willing to stay provided the lifeboat remained alongside.

From what could be gathered they were weary to the point of exhaustion, and were frightened the tow line would part again, as without power they had been unable to secure it properly, and it was in danger of chafing through.

All the afternoon we plodded towards the Sunk in a heavy sea and wind, now at force 8. No word was heard of the tug requested to tow the little ship to safety, and the latter apparently no longer had any means of anchoring.

Finally, in failing light about five miles from the Sunk Lightship, the tow line parted and the lifeboat signalled that he was taking the crew off and heading for shelter. Reluctantly the captain ordered the broken tow rope to be hove in, and after sending out a navigational warning by radio, giving the position of the little derelict, we turned and headed at full speed for Hull.

The *Success* was a very small and probably not very valuable coaster. In terms of commercial salvage, she was not worth very much, particularly as she was empty.

The Law requires the master of any ship to render assistance where life is in danger. The *Esso Cadillac* was the nearest ship able to assist, and the master did his best to save the ship and crew. Perhaps the tow line could have been reconnected, but this would have meant putting the crew at risk and launching a boat — hardly justified in the circumstances when the ship's crew had abandoned the vessel, and no tug had been sent by the owners.

(*above*) The cargo of the *Bretagne* wet and soggy, much of it damaged by sea water and mud.

(*below*) The tug *Noord Holland* — a worthy successor to a famous name in salvage.

(*above*) The *Krab*, a modern salvage vessel used for commercial work, repairing a buoy used for loading oil tankers.

(*below*) The forward half of the *Nyon* which was abandoned and later destroyed completely during a gale.

Cutting the *Nyon* in half. The delicate art of ship surgery.

(*above*) The collision damage and fire raked hull of the *Olympic Thunder*.
(*below*) Tug *Nestor* alongside the *Olympic Thunder* while the other tugs tow her towards Rotterdam.

(*above*) The two halves of the *Olympic Thunder* under repair.
(*below*) The little tug *Junior* proceeding towards the stranded *Esso Peru*.

(*above*) *Santa Kyriaki* being driven ashore by gale force winds.

(*below*) *Mare Nostrum* about to enter the Suez Canal en route to repairs in Europe.

(*above*) *Bretagne* lying on her port side in Ijmuiden harbour.

(*below*) *Bretagne*. Salvage work underway. Note the hole cut in the ship's side to give access to the engine room.

(*above*) Under leaden skies the salvage team of tugs and lifting craft attempt to right the *Bretagne*, assisted by powerful winches mounted on the muddy foreshore.

(*below*) *President Garcia* well and truly aground.

(*above*) The tug *Willem Barendsz*. Another famous name in the world of salvage tugs.

(*below*) *Torrey Canyon* — the sad end of a brave ship.

(*above*) The *Torrey Canyon* – breaking up.

(*below*) Transferring a runner to the *Etnefjell* in the stormy North Atlantic.

(*above*) The tug *Groningen* – an effective salvage tool in several salvage episodes related in this book.

(*below*) *Elwood Mead* held fast on the reefs.

Elwood Mead with decks awash.

(*above*) *Terushima Maru* – Singapore.

(*below*) The *Terushima Maru*, up from the seabed 80 feet below.

(*above*) Lifting the dredger *Mistral*.

(*below*) Large blocks and tackle used for the ground tackle on the *Amagi Maru*.

The oil rig *Orion* mounted piggyback on the barge *Federal 400–2* high and dry on the rocks at low water.

The *Typhoon's* towline breaks but the *Groningen* continues to pull the rig seaward and clear of the barge.

5   The salvage of the m.v. *Nyon*, 4956 g.r.t.

'Half a ship is better than none'

The m.v. *Nyon* was a dry cargo ship under the Swiss flag. On the 15th of November 1958, while in ballast and bound for Dakar from Leith, she ran aground on a rocky part of the coast near Saint Abbs Head at 1906 hours.

The grounding took place approximately $1\frac{1}{2}$ hours after high water. The receding tide left the ship nearly broadside to the cliffs and the forward part of the vessel resting on the three main ridges of rock, which ran more or less at right angles to the fore and aft line in way of No. 2 and 2A holds.

Soundings showed that the stern of the vessel was in deep water which extended to a point just aft of the bridge. The master and crew of the *Nyon* ascertained that the vessel was badly damaged and unlikely to refloat without assistance, and notified their owners accordingly.

The crew, under the direction of the master, set about making temporary repairs in the forward part of the vessel, with the object of reducing and even stopping the water from entering the forward holds. These efforts were doomed to failure, as the crew used wooden plugs and cement. The cement did not have time to set and the working of the metal plates as first the tide receded and then started to rise, broke up the cement and left many of the wooden plugs and battens loose enough to be washed out by the incoming water.

The ship's pumps were kept busy sucking the water out of the damaged holds, but it soon became clear that the pumps did not have the capacity to control the inflow of water as the tide came in. The crew kept up their attempts to plug leaks on successive falling tides and through the low water period, but it was found that the double bottom tank tops were buckling just forward of the deep tanks, and the side plating was also under stress. The weather was good, and though the metal plates worked and made grounding noises on the rocks, there was no heavy pounding.

By the morning of the 16th it was quite clear to those on board that there was a real danger of the ship breaking in two as the tide rose and fell and the after part of the ship became buoyant. The ominous buckling in the tank top plating and side plating showed where the weak point was, and the tide was working the forward and after parts of the ship in much the same way as a door works on hinges.

Meanwhile, the owners of the *Nyon* had been busy. They retained the services of Messrs. France Fenwick, Tyne & Wear Co. Ltd. by signing Lloyd's Open Form, and this company dispatched the tugs *George V* and *Beamish*, which arrived on the scene at 0625 and 0730 respectively on the 16th of November.

The *George V* actually put a rope on board the *Nyon*, but was not permitted to tow by her master who feared that the strain might cause the buckled plating to fracture and split the ship in two. The ship's distress signals had been picked up by Bureau Wijsmuller and the tugs *Simson* and *Hector* were dispatched immediately with heavy pumps, divers and a quantity of salvage equipment.

At the same time, two Wijsmuller salvage inspectors left for Edinburgh by air. At 1200 on the 17th, the master of the *Nyon* accepted the services of Bureau Wijsmuller on Lloyd's Open Form.

A conference was held between representatives of the two salvage companies and the ship, regarding the best method of refloating. At this meeting it was decided that the leakage in forward holds would have to be brought under control, and that the best way to handle this was to put on board sufficient portable pumps. The *Beamish* had been dispatched to Rosyth to pick up some British Admiralty pumps and returned on the 17th at 1635 with three 6-inch portable pumps which were installed in the 'tween decks of forward holds.

At 2020 the Wijsmuller tug *Simson* arrived and put one 3-inch motor driven, and two electric pumps on board to be installed in the 'tween decks of leaking holds. At 2020 on the 18th the *Hector* arrived and placed one 4-inch and four 3-inch portable pumps on board.

Largely because the buckling and bottom damage increased as time went by, the efforts of crew and salvors to plug the leaks and control the inflow of water with portable pumps failed. An attempt to tow the vessel off with the *George V* and the *Simson* on the morning of the 18th was abandoned before either tug took the strain seriously.

It was decided not to give up the principle of controlling the water with pumps, and tugs were dispatched for more and better ones. The *George V* and the *Beamish* went off to the Forth and returned with six 6-inch motor pumps and a quantity of salvage material to help repair the leaks. While they were putting the pumps on board during the afternoon of the 19th, it was noted that a ground swell was present and the tugs were ranging and bumping slightly, and later the vessel began to work as the tide rose.

At 2130 the tug *Simson* returned from shore with two high speed 350 T.P.H. pumps, which had been flown up from London, and additional repair equipment. Gradually the experts were being forced to the conclusion that the forepart of the ship would have to be abandoned and the ship cut in two.

On the 20th of November at 1200 hours, five days after the ship had gone aground, the owners and both salvors agreed to cut her in two pieces and twenty three of the crew of thirty three were sent ashore.

All the salvage pumps and equipment had to be recovered by the tugs, and the *George V* went off to Rosyth to land her pumps and collect cutting equipment. The next thirty six hours were used in strengthening the engine room and deep tank bulkhead, sealing pipes and preparing to cut the vessel's hull, decks and double bottom tank tops, as well as removing the more valuable equipment from the fore-section.

During the afternoon of the 22nd, the cutting work commenced and about three quarters of the total width of the ship was completed before the incoming tide stopped work.

On the 23rd at 0530, cutting was resumed and the *Hector* and *George V* were made fast aft. As the cutting continued and the tide rose, the two tugs commenced towing and the *Hector* and *Beamish* hooked up to their sister ships to increase the pull. The first attempt to separate the two halves of the vessel failed, and another attempt on the 24th also failed to produce the desired effect.

The vessel had been aground nine days by this time, and the weather had been very good for the time of year. The experts from both salvage companies were aware that it couldn't last, and decided to use explosive charges. Accordingly, the *Beamish* went off to Rosyth to pick up the explosives, and returned with the charges early on the 25th.

The first charges were placed and exploded on the 25th at 0800, and again during the evening at low water on the 26th. Neither the explosives nor the towing action of the tugs was successful in freeing the vessel. On the 27th more charges were fired, and the tugs kept up the necessary strain on the after part as and when required. The swell was increasing and at about 1500 on the 27th it became evident that the remaining plates holding the two parts of the ship together were at last beginning to give. The swell assisted the rising tide and gradually the after section rose so that the deck was five or six feet above the corresponding section of deck on the fore part of the vessel.

After high water as the tide dropped, the stern half of the vessel moved suddenly as the final separation occurred, assisted by the strain exerted by all four tugs. Once afloat it was found that the after section floated safely, thanks to the strengthening work done by the salvage teams in the deep tanks and engine room.

The *Hector* and *George V* towed the stern half of the *Nyon* to the Tyne, which was reached safely at 0815 on the 28th of November, and handed the ship over to the harbour tugs. The fore part of the *Nyon* was destroyed totally in a gale a few days later. The stern half, after strengthening, was towed to Bolnes in Holland where a new bow section was fitted, and the vessel returned to normal service in the autumn of 1959.

The salvage, or partial salvage, of the *Nyon* is interesting for more than one reason. The big question was – could the entire ship have been saved? Looking back, it is easy to be wise and provide ready made solutions that would in theory at least have done the job. In practice, an honest answer to such a question must be 'Probably not, with the time and equipment available'.

Approximately thirteen days elapsed between the *Nyon* running aground and the delivery of the after section safely to the Tyne. In the second half of November the weather was extraordinarily good for the area and all concerned were extremely lucky. Events proved that attempting to seal the leaks in the fore part of the vessel and to control the water there with portable pumps, were largely non-productive and lost more than five days, which might have been critical if the weather had deteriorated.

With two salvage companies involved and the owner reluctant to agree to such a drastic step as cutting the vessel in half without first trying to save the whole ship, the delay is understandable.

It is apparent that both salvors worked together in the best interests of the client and that each successive step was taken with the full agreement of all parties. The *Nyon*, when she went ashore, had no cargo on board. There is no doubt that cutting the vessel in half saved the most valuable part, including the main engine and other machinery.

The value of the salvaged section of the ship was agreed at
£145,000 and the salvors received £58,000 shared equally between
them.

6 The salvage of the *Olympic Thunder*

During the night of the 25th/26th of April 1962, the Liberian tanker *Olympic Thunder* was in collision with the Greek ship *Kissavos*. As a result of the collision the *Olympic Thunder* had a series of explosions in her cargo tanks which caused considerable damage, and resulted in the vessel catching fire amidships.

The crew of *Olympic Thunder* abandoned ship and were rescued by a fishing vessel which was in the vicinity of the disaster. Following distress messages, a number of tugs were dispatched to the assistance of the burning vessel which had given its position as Latitude 53° 56′ North, Longitude 3° 20′ East.

The weather in the area was good with light winds and calm seas, but a great deal of fog was present, particularly in coastal areas. Among the tugs which were sent to the aid of the distressed ship was the German tug *Wotan* owned by Bugsier. The Dutch tugs *Holland* and *Doggersbank*, owned by Doeksen, and the Wijsmuller tugs *Titan*, *Simson*, *Friesland* and *Nestor*. All the tugs had to contend with a great deal of fog, as they proceeded towards the burning ship, which made the risk of grounding and collision serious.

Meanwhile, Bureau Wijsmuller and Messrs. Doeksen had come to an agreement whereby a joint salvage contract had been signed. Mr. Doeksen Jr. was to have overall control of the salvage operation and the Wijsmuller salvage inspector T. P. Hoek would direct his tugs and fire fighting teams after consulting with him.

The tugs began to arrive in the vicinity of the stricken vessel about 1700 hours on the 26th, and commenced fighting the fire by spraying water jets on the burning ship. Initially the tugs *Titan* and *Holland* worked from the starboard side of the ship, while the *Simson*, *Doggersbank* and *Nestor* worked from the port side. The *Wotan* and *Friesland* stood by to render assistance if required. The task was a dual one, to attack the fire in the midship accommodation and paint stores, and to cool the tanks to try to avoid further explosions and the risk of the fire spreading.

The tug crews had put small parties of fire fighters on board, but after assessing the situation, the two salvage inspectors agreed a joint plan whereby most of the crews returned to their tugs and a special fire fighting squad, equipped with fire fighting suits, smoke masks and helmets brought out by the *Nestor*, took over. This squad, using breathing apparatus and equipped with fire axes, brought to bear six additional hoses operated from a six-cylinder portable pump, also brought out by the *Nestor*.

To start with, the fire squad concentrated on the store rooms and paint locker which were burning fiercely. Dry powder chemical was sprayed in the store rooms, then followed up with water sprays.

The master of the *Olympic Thunder* was anxious to recover the contents of his safe which contained a number of documents and a great deal of money. Using breathing apparatus and chemical fire extinguishers, two members of the squad fought their way through the flames putting out the fire as they went, with such success that the master was able to enter his room which had been gutted by fire and, after some initial difficulty, opened his safe and removed the contents unharmed.

By 1900 the fires were under control as a result of the combined efforts of the tugs and fire fighters on board the ship, and preparation was made to tow the vessel. While some of the tugs continued to spray water over the smouldering midship superstructure and hull, the *Holland* made fast her towing wire on the starboard bow, and the *Titan* on the port bow. 'Not Under Command' lights were rigged on the bridge of the *Olympic Thunder*, as well as the green and red sidelights.

A plan was agreed by which the *Nestor* would remain alongside the ship to support the fire fighting squad which was still putting out fires in the accommodation, but the *Simson* and *Doggersbank* recovered their equipment and cast off before making fast to their sister ships so that all four tugs could be used to tow in tandem.

The force of the collision and subsequent explosions had weakened the vessel amidship, and there was some fear that the slight ground swell might break her in two unless care was taken to tow her slowly.

At 2020 the tow commenced with the weather gradually deteriorating. By midnight the *Nestor* which was ranging and rolling alongside, had to let go, but not before one lifeboat was smashed and a number of ropes broken. The tow continued at slow speed, without major incident towards Rotterdam. At 1805 on the 27th, in the vicinity of the Fairway Buoy, the *Simson* and *Doggersbank* cast off and then made fast aft for the passage into the port.

Pilots were put on each tug, and the harbour master boarded the *Olympic Thunder* to inspect the ship prior to permitting her to enter. Finally, permission was given and she was towed to a berth at the tank cleaning station to enable her to be gas freed and cleaned, before repairs.

The *Olympic Thunder* was drydocked and subsequently enlarged, and re-entered normal service at the end of 1963.

Fire on an oil tanker is always a dangerous affair. This is particularly true if the vessel is not equipped with an inert gas system, and happens to be in ballast in a non-gas-free condition. In 1962 few tankers were fitted with inert gas systems, and the tug crews who fought this fire were in very considerable danger. The operation was a model combined operation in which the two salvage companies operated well together.

The special equipment and fire fighting squad supplied by the *Nestor* were key factors in getting the fire under control and keeping it out. The risk of the ship breaking in two was probably realistic, but with the number of tugs present both halves would undoubtedly have floated and been saved.

7 The stranding and salvage of the *Esso Deutschland* at Marsa el Brega, Libya

The serious matter of stranding can frequently be disastrous if a vessel goes ashore on a rocky coastline and runs the risk of being pounded to pieces by heavy seas. In the case of an oil tanker, the situation can be further complicated if the vessel is loaded, as there is always a danger of the cargo leaking, with increased risk of fire and pollution.

The hazards involved to crew and salvors, as well as environmental considerations make all such salvage operations of interest, as the methods used can be analysed in terms of success or failure, and where applicable can be used again with the necessary modifications to meet a new set of requirements.

The *Esso Deutschland*, 94,650 d.w.t., belonged to Esso Tankschiff Reederei. Built in 1963, she was two years old at the time this incident occurred. A fine modern vessel, she and her sister ship the *Esso Bayern* were the two largest ships belonging to Esso Tankschiff. They were also two of the largest tankers under the German flag at the time.

The *Esso Deutschland* had called at Marsa el Brega to load a cargo of crude oil. She arrived off the port at 1212 hours on the 24th of November 1965, and on obtaining a pilot, berthed at the No. 4 seaberth at 1518 on the same day. For those not familiar with offshore loading ports, it should be explained that Marsa el Brega is a port which includes an offshore terminal, owned and operated by Esso Standard Libya Inc. At that time there were four individual crude oil loading facilities, all of them offshore and in the open sea, unprotected by any breakwaters or harbour works.

Three of the four loading facilities consist of multi-buoy seaberths to which the tanker secures after dropping both anchors, in such a position that her bow is secured by her anchors and the stern by mooring wires to the mooring buoys – five in the small berths, and seven in No. 4 berth.

Each vessel has to be positioned precisely, so that she can pick up the two submarine hoses and connect them to her midship cargo manifold. After deballasting, crude oil is loaded into the vessel from shore by means of a submarine pipeline. The rate is controlled and adjusted by the operators on shore to the ship's requirements, and communication is by V.H.F. radio. Obviously, mooring and loading large tankers at such exposed facilities depends on reasonable weather conditions. Bad weather with strong winds and rough seas, not only prevents oil tankers from berthing but can also make it necessary for them to leave prior to the completion of loading.

The *Esso Deutschland* berthed in good weather, and after discharging her ballast commenced loading crude oil at 1200. In addition, two other vessels were loading crude oil in the port – the *World Beauty* and *Silver Springs*, both vessels considerably smaller than the *Esso Deutschland*.

During the night the weather deteriorated with little or no warning and all three ships were caught still loading. In a situation such as this, the decision to leave or stay in the berth remains with the master of the ship, who depends heavily on the advice of his skilled mooring master, or pilot.

Letting go moorings in the open sea requires a mooring boat with a skilled crew, but there is considerable risk to the boat and crew in such an unmooring operation, particularly at night. In addition, a big tanker is harder to handle when she is flying light and unmooring in strong winds and rough seas.

Each of the three vessels concerned elected to stay in their berths to continue loading, but by 0446 the *Esso Deutschland* was having problems with moorings breaking, and stopped loading.

The wind was now 40 knots, with a rough sea and increasing swell. The marine superintendent discussed the situation with the master and pilot on the radio, and it was agreed that the vessel would have to leave the berth prior to completing cargo and that loading should continue till daylight in view of the risk of trying to unmoor and leave in the dark. Loading was resumed, and finally stopped at 0717, after which the vessel disconnected the hoses and prepared to leave the berth.

By 0921 hours on the 25th of November, the *Esso Deutschland* had been successfully unmoored and commenced to work ahead, heaving on her port anchor and using her engines to ease the strain on the port anchor chain. At 0949 the port anchor was hove clear of the water, and she commenced manoeuvring to ease the strain, while heaving on the starboard anchor chain.

Things started to go wrong about this time. Between 0949 and

1002, the vessel appeared to have gone out of control and gradually went down to leeward inspite of all efforts to stop it.

Long afterwards it was discovered that one fluke had broken off the starboard anchor, and this may go some way to explaining why the vessel dragged down to leeward and did not respond in the normal way to port helm and ahead engine movements. By 1002 the stern and screw were foul of No. 7 mooring buoy, and fifty eight minutes later, at exactly 1100, the vessel was aground – despite the fact that the port anchor and then the stern anchor were let go in a desperate attempt to save her. It is a matter of interest that the *World Beauty* left with a full cargo at 0725. The *Silver Springs* departed at 1210 with a full cargo, though the mooring master was unable to get off the latter ship due to heavy seas.

An accident such as this is a major catastrophe no matter where it happens. In Libya, with the somewhat limited resources of a small port, the problem is even more acute. To evaluate the situation, the marine superintendent made an attempt to get on board from the small Wijsmuller tug *Junior* which, together with the larger tug *Cycloop*, were under contract to assist ships using Marsa el Brega, and were prohibited by contract from claiming salvage in the port area.

The *Esso Deutschland* was lying almost broadside to the wind and sea, with heavy seas pounding her and sometimes sweeping across the main deck. It took a lot of skill and judgement on the part of the *Junior's* master to make the headlong dash around the ship's bow to the relative calm of the lee side. Once he was safely on board, *Junior* made another wild dash for open water and, half submerged at times, finally made it to the open sea, and thence to shelter behind the small harbour breakwater.

Conditions on the big ship were grave. By 1225, both the forward anchor chains had parted and she shuddered continuously as the heavy seas struck. The master was a worried man, but behaved in a calm and dignified manner. He and his crew were to prove able in all aspects of seamanship which conditions demanded, and the discipline on board was in keeping with the high standard associated with the German merchant marine.

It became evident that nothing could be done, either on board or ashore, to get the ship off while the gale lasted. A real danger existed that the ship would start to break up, and in doing so, all or part of her cargo would be lost to the sea, with all that that implied in terms of fire hazard and/or extensive pollution in the port area. After discussing the situation with the master, it was decided:

i)   To sound round the ship and to fix her outline on a large scale hydrographic chart in the port office ashore. From this, it could be determined what type of bottom could be expected round the ship, and the depth of water. Fixing the vessel was double checked, from shore and ship, and the coordinates when plotted showed that she had grounded in a fairly level area with depths of 30–35 feet. The least depth was on the leeward side, just forward of the midship manifold.

ii)   After discussing the situation, it was mutually agreed that the seabed in the immediate vicinity of the ship appeared to be mainly sand, and that it might help the vessel to gravitate in some ballast to fix her firmly in position and prevent her from working. Ballast was gravitated into the permanent ballast tanks between 1800 and 1820, and as a result the ship appeared to be a lot easier.

From the practical standpoint, all that could be done on board had been done to preserve the vessel intact. The next step was to plan ahead, with a view to getting her off when the weather improved. The owners in Hamburg had been informed of the casualty by radio, and the master was told that he should not agree to any contract or commitment without approval from Hamburg. Meanwhile, the owners were flying a representative out to Marsa el Brega with authority to act for them.

It became apparent that several large and small salvage tugs were heading towards Marsa el Brega in the hopes of salvage. Offers of assistance were also received from oil companies and other sources in Libya. On board the ship, the master and Esso Libya's marine superintendent reviewed the situation. It became increasingly clear that some of the 60,000 tons of crude oil on board the ship would have to be removed if the vessel was to be refloated quickly and without further damage.

An official request was sent to Esso's head office asking for a tanker to be allocated for this purpose, the idea being to use a smaller ship to take off at least 15,000 tons of the crude oil. Most of the night was spent in planning and discussing with port control and the management of Esso Standard, Libya, how best the manpower, harbour craft and other equipment could be utilised, first to refloat the *Esso Deutschland*, and second to resume the shipment of crude oil when the weather improved.

Recollections of that long night are still something of a nightmare. The hours of waiting were broken by intermittent cups of coffee, brief conversations on the V.H.F. radio with the port office and endless attempts to ease mental and physical stress, first by walking up and down and then sitting in one place and another, while listening to the whistling of the wind and the working of the ship, trying to detect some reduction in the malignant forces around her.

In the waiting hours under such conditions, sleep was impossible. Nobody was any longer consciously frightened for their personal safety, but inevitably conversation became impossible.

As daylight arrived, so the weather started to improve. The port office came on the air with the information that the *Esso Denmark*, a 34,600 d.w.t. tanker, had been diverted and was heading towards Marsa el Brega to assist. With this good news, things seemed to take a turn for the better, and the wind and sea started to subside gradually. By 0715 on the 26th, the marine superintendent was able to leave the *Esso Deutschland* to get the port working again.

By noon the port was open and ships were being berthed and loaded as if nothing had happened, but in fact a major effort was underway to refloat the *Esso Deutschland*.

A flood of messages showed that several salvage tugs were due, and it became apparent to the management of Esso Libya that the activities of tugs and others would have to be coordinated if the operation was to be brought to a successful conclusion and the normal port operations were not to be interfered with unduly.

The marine superintendent volunteered to act as salvage master, and the owners agreed to accept him in this capacity. At the request of Esso Libya, he prepared two alternative plans to lighten the *Esso Deutschland* and to tow her off. In addition, a third plan was laid out by Esso Libya's Engineering Group should either or both of the other plans, which involved the use of the *Esso Denmark*, fail. As frequently happens in the Gulf of Sidra once a gale blows itself out, the wind and sea dropped remarkably quickly, leaving a long swell from the north which only subsided gradually.

The first plan involved taking the *Esso Denmark* alongside the *Esso Deutschland* and offloading about 15,000 tons of crude oil. This would require the swell to subside, as the *Esso Denmark* would

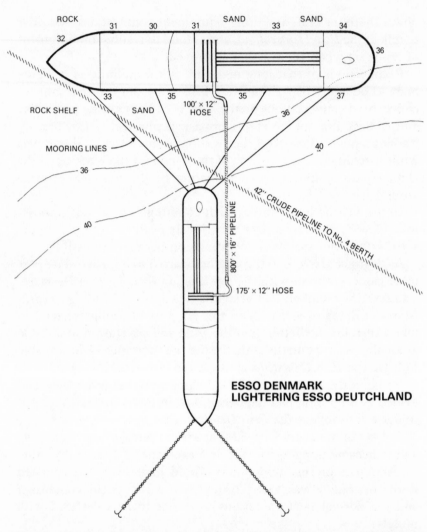

have to lie alongside the other during the transhipment. The plan also called for the use of several tugs to reduce the risk of heavy contact while berthing and unberthing. In turn this meant that any outside tugs used would be able to claim salvage.

The second plan involved the use of 800 feet of 16-inch pipe, fitted with 100 feet of 12-inch hose on one end and 175 feet on the other. This plan visualised the *Esso Denmark* mooring stern to the *Esso Deutschland,* but several hundred feet away and with her anchors out forward as if she was in a seaberth.

Such a plan required the pipe and hose to be welded together ashore and launched, then towed out on the surface and sunk precisely in position. The drawback was the time required to assemble and weld the pipe, and to rig the hoses. The management of Esso Libya decided to build the pipeline and have everything ready regardless of whether it was used, and a crash construction pro- gramme was organised. This second plan had the advantage that once the pipeline was sunk in position, the *Esso Denmark* could moor and discharge regardless of the swell, and as she would be in deeper water could take more than 15,000 tons if necessary. In addition it would not require the use of any outside tugs, as she could moor with the help of the *Cycloop* and two mooring boats.

Both plans were discussed with the masters of the two ships, and both regarded plan No. 2 as a first choice, as it removed contact between the ships and reduced the risk of damage, fire and pollu- tion. The owner's representative, who arrived from Hamburg on the 26th of November, also approved this plan.

It became clear in reviewing all the factors involved, that the construction of the pipeline was going to dictate the timetable. The best estimates indicated that it would be ready for launching at 1600 hours on the 27th, and available for use about two hours later. This meant it might not be available for sinking before dark on the 27th of November. With these thoughts in mind it was decided to be prepared to switch to plan No. 1 if anything went wrong or further delays occurred which would not permit the transhipment to start before sunset on the 27th.

At 0820 hours on the 27th, the marine superintendent once again boarded the *Esso Deutschland* and found the swell still 3–4 feet high, which made plan No. 1 a high risk but, just in case, the tug *Cycloop* was ordered to take out one 50-foot, and four 25-foot lengths of 12-inch hose. In addition, it was judged that divers would be able to work on the lee side of the ship and inspect the propeller. This inspection was successful, and the propeller and rudder were found to be free.

The rest of the morning was spent in going over the calculations. It was agreed that about 4 feet of lift was required, which would mean transhipping 15,000 tons. In addition it was decided to take on 15,000 tons of ballast while this transfer was taking place, so that the vessel would not float off before we were ready for her.

Ashore, things were going well – beyond the best expectations – and at 1115 hours the *L4* derrick barge and the tug *Junior* com- menced pulling the pipe into the water. At 1535 the whole assembly, complete with hoses, was ready for towing to the *Esso Deutschland*. The progress made in getting the pipe ready necessitated a slight adjustment to the original plan, and with the agreement of all concerned it was decided to moor the *Esso Denmark* prior to positioning and sinking the pipe.

At 1430 hours Esso Libya's marine superintendent boarded the *Esso Denmark*, and at 1530 the anchor was weighed. Assisted by the tug *Cycloop* she moved into position and dropped each anchor on a pre-arranged spot, marked by small buoys, then proceeded to moor stern towards the *Esso Deutschland*. By 1650 the *Denmark* was moored in position, and at 1720 *Junior* assisted by the workboat *Jebel*, arrived towing the pipe. By 1914 hours one end of the hose and pipe was secured on board *Deutschland*, while the other was towed alongside *Denmark*.

Now began the critical task of flooding the pipe and sinking it to the bottom. If the pipe buckled and ruptured, all the work would have been in vain. Fortunately, everything went well, and at 2040 hours it was safely on the bottom. At 2050 the hose on the other end was hauled aboard the *Denmark* and connected up. The next step was to test the hoses and line, and this was done by pumping water from the *Denmark* to the *Deutschland*.

At 2248 hours on the 27th, the *Deutschland* commenced discharging crude oil to the *Denmark*, an operation which continued all night until 1036 hours on the 28th, when it was thought that sufficient oil had been transferred. Next the hose and pipe were cleared of oil, to avoid pollution when disconnected, by pumping water from the *Denmark* through the pipe, fast enough to displace all the oil.

At 1107 hours, water pumping was stopped and the hoses on both ships disconnected, blanked off and lowered to the seabed. At daylight on the 28th, the swell was nearly gone and it was decided to try to move the barge *L4* out to the *Deutschland* to assist in transferring her stern anchor and chain to the starboard bow to provide her with a means of anchoring once she was afloat.

The *L4* carried out this work between 0900 hours and 1300, while *Deutschland* was pumping out her clean ballast. At 1400 the *Denmark*, with her anchors still out forward, let go her port quarter moorings and repositioned slightly with towing lines secured to the bow of the *Deutschland*. At 1430 the *Cycloop* made fast to the stern of the *Deutschland*, and the *Junior* stood by on the lee side to push.

At 1700 hours the *Deutschland* began to move a little, and *Denmark* commenced to heave in her anchors and exert a little pressure on the tow line.

At 1748 hours the vessel was afloat fore and aft and being towed clear.

A little later the *Cycloop* let go aft, and *Denmark* released the *Esso Deutschland*, the latter vessel proceeding to the anchorage under her own power.

The marine superintendent disembarked from the *Denmark* at 1815 and this vessel also went to anchor. No oil was lost, and even the hoses and pipe were eventually blown to the surface and recovered.

As salvage operations go, the use of a pipeline and hoses in the manner described is possibly unique, and probably saved time and risk of dangerous contact between the lightering vessel and the grounded tanker. Using the *Esso Denmark* and the contract Wijsmuller tugs, avoided the use of outside tugs and salvage claims from such craft.

8   The stranding and refloating of the *Esso Peru*

Open roadsteads are frequently the sites of accidents or major marine disasters. During the last century, a fleet of sailing ships were wrecked off Dover in the Downs during a severe storm. The close proximity of a large number of vessels made collision inevitable as anchors dragged and individual ships fought to get under way and clear of the shoals.

In more recent times the dangers and difficulties may not appear to be as great, but changes in the weather can be sudden and, unless prepared to get under way and steam out to the open sea, a modern high powered ship can soon be in trouble.

On the 12th of December 1965, this is exactly what happened to the 52,000 d.w.t. tanker *Esso Peru*, which had anchored awaiting a loading berth 1½ miles east of the Marsa el Brega sea buoy. During the previous day, strong offshore winds had been experienced which had reduced visibility close to the coast, due to the amount of sand in the air. As frequently happens, the sea remained relatively unruffled, and as night fell and the wind dropped, it became the shimmering blue mirror so often seen in the travel brochure. For those unaware of the symptoms and significance of a low barometer in the Gulf of Sidra, it looks as if the unsettled weather has moved on.

In fact, it is the calm before the storm front, which arrives with little or no warning, with winds from the west or west north west sometimes gusting to 65 and 70 knots, and doing appalling damage afloat and ashore in the space of a few minutes. The passage of such a frontal system is followed by a rapid increase in wave height, the wind whipping the waves and causing short steep seas which can be particularly dangerous for small craft.

Under these conditions at Brega, in approximately 8 hours the waves reach 10 feet, measured trough to crest. If the wind persists in strength and gradually veers to north west and north, within twelve hours the seas are 10 to 15 feet and the whole coastline and outlying reefs are covered by endless rows of breakers marching with military precision to their doom on the sandy beaches or submerged coral reefs. The noise of the breakers gradually swells from a low mutter to a roar which is particularly sinister at night, but even in daylight tends to transcend the normal sounds of every day life in the port.

On this occasion, the seaberths had been closed and all ships waiting off the port had been warned of impending bad weather, but a number of them, including the *Esso Peru* and the dry cargo ship *Cattaro*, chose to remain at anchor.

The decision to remain at anchor in such circumstances is up to the individual master. Those with experience of the sealine terminals in the Gulf of Sidra know that conditions can change in a few hours, and are careful to have their engines on standby, proceeding out into deep water the minute the weather changes. Those with less experience or subject to other pressures, such as a limited amount of bunker fuel on board, are reluctant to go to sea, and under such circumstances tend to remain at anchor till the anchors start to drag, or the conditions become completely untenable.

At 0340 hours on the 12th of December, the port control office at Brega received a call from the *Esso Peru* stating that she was going full speed ahead but was making no progress, and requesting assistance from the tug *Cycloop*. The wind was from the west, and the speed indicator was showing a steady 40 knots. It is possible that the readings obtained in the port office were on the low side, as high ground and buildings tended to shelter the instrument.

The marine superintendent was notified of the distress call and gave instructions to put the Wijsmuller tug on standby so that she could put to sea if this was safe and feasible. However, her master had very serious doubts that the tug had the power to leave the shelter of the breakwater and pass up the buoyed channel between the reefs with the heavy sea and gale force winds on the beam. It was finally agreed that it would be unwise to attempt to leave in the dark, and that they would take another look at the situation at dawn.

At 0512 the cargo ship *Cattaro* stated that she was dragging anchor and required assistance. Both vessels were informed that the *Cycloop* would try to reach them at first light, but neither vessel replied. At 0630 the tug left harbour, disappeared round the end of the breakwater, and was lost to sight in the half light and heavy seas which filled the air with spray and spindrift. Wind was still from the west blowing 45–48 knots.

At 0700 the light had improved and the *Cycloop* reported that the *Cattaro* had slipped her anchor and chain and had proceeded to sea, but the *Esso Peru* appeared to be still at anchor between the shore and Magdar Reef, but there was no contact on V.H.F. or W/T.

At 0730 *Esso Peru* was heard again calling for assistance and contact was established by V.H.F. She reported that her steering gear was unusable, but visual inspection indicated nothing wrong with the rudder. Contact was spasmodic, but she stated that she was using her engines at reduced power due to sand in the condenser.

At 0830 contact was again made with the ship, and she gave her position as 1 mile north of Magdar Point, indicating that she was still afloat and lying to four shackles on each anchor between the reef and the shore. A message was passed to the effect that if she dragged her anchors and went aground, the crew should run ballast into the ship to steady her, and stop the breakers from driving her into too shallow water, from which it would be difficult to refloat her when the weather moderated.

At 0900 the management of Esso Standard Libya suggested that an attempt be made to establish a shore watch at a point directly on shore from the *Esso Peru*, and that this shore watch be equipped with a portable radio and first aid equipment in case the vessel broke up.

By 0945, the shore station had been set up, consisting of four men and two Land Rovers, as well as a portable radio. This had entailed driving outside the camp and the perimeter fence and across 3 or 4 miles of rough desert terrain to a desolate part of the coast that had not been properly cleared of mines from World War II. Arrangements were made to change the men every eight hours and to maintain the watch indefinitely.

The *Cycloop* reported that she could see the ship beyond the reef, but due to sea conditions could not pass through the reef to help her, and was therefore returning to harbour. The shore watch party reported every hour to port control that there was no change in the situation, but at 1647 the wind, now west north west, gusted to 58 knots during a squall, and the shore watch said the vessel might have grounded.

At 1712 the shore party reported that the ship's anchor chains were running out and that they could see a cloud of rust and dirt on the forecastle.

At 1715 the *Esso Peru* reported she was aground aft, and had 9 shackles on each anchor.

At 1730 the master asked if it was advisable to pump in more ballast, and was told to do so as the shore party indicated that the ship was rolling 10 degrees from the vertical. They also felt that she was gradually moving south along the shore. Failing light and heavy rain squalls made it impossible to see exactly what was happening, but the ship was now rolling up to 15 degrees and yawing. Communication was not reliable, and the vessel's V.H.F. set seemed to be shut down other than when they wanted to contact port control.

At 2145 the shore party indicated that the ship had definitely moved south and west, and was getting closer to Magdar Point and the company's perimeter fence. At 0145 on the 13th of December, *Esso Peru* came on the air and indicated that the weather was moderating. The master also stated that he had been in radio contact with his owners and had been instructed to contact the marine superintendent at Brega to obtain assistance refloating. He was requested by his owners to 'Try to minimise the damage!'

In the course of this conversation, the master reported that his steering gear was out of action, but the main engine was working and he had 10 shackles out on each anchor. The extent of bottom damage was unknown, but there was no water in the engine room. During the rest of the night the weather continued to moderate and the shore watch reported no change in the situation. At 0945 they packed up and drove back across the desert to take up a new position just inside the company's fence.

With the improvement in the weather it became necessary to organise manpower and craft to refloat the *Esso Peru*, and to consider opening the port to resume the shipment of crude oil. The first step was to accurately fix the position of the ship, and to put her outline on a large scale survey.

By 1015 this had been done and the ship's position was fixed as 2.95 miles on 066°T (true) from the end of the Brega breakwater. Examination of the charts and surveys revealed that she was now aground south of Magdar Reef and inside Brega Bay, in a location where the bottom would consist of sand.

At 1115, V.H.F. contact was established with *Esso Peru*, and arrangements made for a regular radio schedule. In addition, the ship indicated that her rudder was damaged and unusable, and the windlass bearings were damaged, but were being repaired. The weather continued to moderate, but remained squally with heavy sea and swell. It seemed that the ship had dragged her anchors on the night of the 11th, and had been driven by big seas across

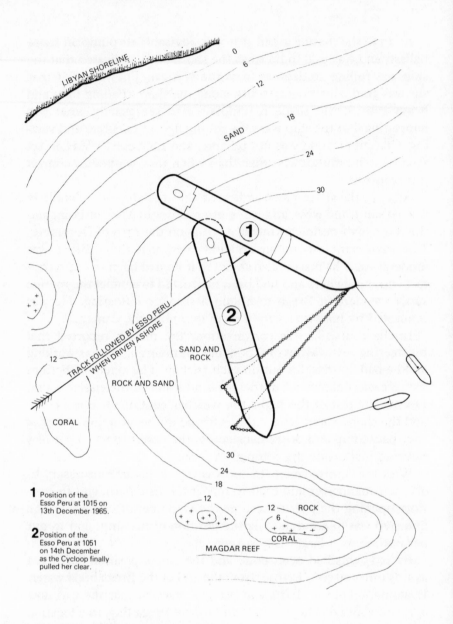

1 Position of the
Esso Peru at 1015 on
13th December 1965.

2 Position of the
Esso Peru at 1051
on 14th December
as the Cycloop finally
pulled her clear.

the outer reef which showed least depths of 6–15 feet over it. She
had then, apparently, remained afloat until about 1700 hours on
the 12th, when the combined force of current, wind and sea had
made her drag her anchors once again. Between 1700 on the 12th
and 1015 on the following day, she had moved down the coast with
her stern sometimes ashore, for a distance of approximately 1½
miles, moving over rock and dead coral patches with less than 12

feet of water over them, until she came to rest actually on a sandy stretch of shore inside Brega Bay.

The ship must, in the course of such a passage, have sustained heavy bottom damage. She was fortunate to have retained her watertight integrity, as the rocks and coral could easily have torn great holes in her bottom.

V.H.F. contact indicated that she had 13,569 tons of ballast on board, and the master thought the vessel would now have a draft of 21 feet 6 inches for'd and 25 feet 6 inches aft, if afloat in salt water.

Though aground aft, the ship's head was yawing between 270° and 295°True on the gyro, and the anchor chains were leading to starboard about 30 to 40 degrees on the bow most of the time. Looking at the survey it did not seem too big a job to refloat the ship as there was deep water on the port bow, and once afloat the vessel could be towed out of the bay by the eastern ship channel. The main problem was the limited amount of working room behind Magdar Reef and the ship's bows, and the limited horsepower of the *Cycloop*. The anchor chains leading to starboard with anchors undoubtedly hooked up in the dead coral or rock outcrops which the ship had so miraculously crossed, might also cause problems.

The squally weather and large swell were still bad enough to keep the port closed and precluded normal operations, so the marine superintendent decided to go and have a look at the situation first hand to see if anything could be done to refloat the vessel. The abnormally high water level and swell could help in the operation.

At 1410 on the 12th the superintendent left the harbour on board the *Cycloop* with the small tug *Junior* and the mooring launch *Delta* in attendance. On approaching the *Esso Peru*, the master of *Cycloop* and the marine superintendent examined the amount of space available to the tug. It was agreed that she could connect up and tow the ship, as long as she remained on the port bow.

A plan was worked out whereby the superintendent would board the ship, and provided her windlass was in working order they would try to ease the vessel off with *Cycloop* heaving on the ship's anchors at the same time.

At 1520 the superintendent transferred to the *Junior*, which went alongside the *Esso Peru*. Once on board, he found the Spanish master and crew shaken and weary. Though aground aft, the ship was rolling and shuddering under the impact of the swell on the starboard bow. He found that the windlass had been repaired, and explained to the master the plan to refloat the ship:

i)   The *Cycloop*'s towing wire would be connected on the port bow.

ii)   The windlass would be put in gear, to heave on both anchors while the tug pulled broad on the port bow to stop the ship's head swinging to starboard and towards the shallows.

iii) Ballast would be pumped out to lighten the ship and assist in refloating her.

The master agreed, and preparations were made on board to secure the tug. At 1623 the starboard anchor chain was put in gear, and the *Esso Peru* commenced heaving. The ship's head was 300°True. The wind north west 26 knots.

At 1641 *Cycloop* reported that she was putting weight on the tow wire and increasing power. The starboard chain was coming in slowly and the ship's head swinging to starboard. At 1647 her head was 301°True and the *Cycloop* was ordered to pull broader on the bow to counter the swing; 3 minutes later it was necessary to stop heaving on the starboard anchor and switch to the port anchor, as a bight of slack cable was fouling the starboard anchor chain.

At 1700 the ship's head was 314°True and she stopped heaving on the port anchor and resumed heaving on the starboard, with the tug still pulling on the port bow at full power.

At 1718 the ship's head was 325°True and at 1730, 340°True with the ship heading right at Magdar Reef, and very little room ahead. There were now 7 shackles on the starboard anchor, and a switch was made to the port anchor to pick up the slack chain, as the two chains were fouling each other. Shortly after, with the light failing, it was thought best to send the *Delta* and *Junior* back to Brega Harbour as they were unable to do much.

At 1810 the two anchor chains were cleared and the marine superintendent tried to persuade the master to heave them tight and reballast the ship for the night, as by then it was too dark to see the reef or what they were doing, but the thought of another night aground was too much for him, and they kept on heaving.

The ship's engines were now tried, first at slow ahead, and then at full ahead, without moving her.

At 1837 the *Cycloop* said it was no longer possible to continue.

He could not make out the edge of the reef clearly, and at 1857 she was let go, and returned to Brega Harbour. On board the *Esso Peru* they calculated that the ship had moved slightly, about 50 yards closer to deep water. They now had 5 and 6½ shackles of chain out on each anchor, and the ship's head was 338° True. It was decided to put 5000 tons of ballast in to steady the ship and stop her pounding. It could be pumped out the next day.

As can be expected, the master and crew were very dejected at having to spend another night aground. Conversation was limited by language and the weary depression that night watches bring on such occasions. The master had not slept since the night of the 10th, which meant he had been over three days without sleep. The superintendent persuaded him to go to bed fully clothed, and he slept with the aid of a sedative.

During the night the weather improved sufficiently to allow the port to be opened again, and tankers to be berthed by daylight.

At 0700 on the 14th, the master and marine superintendent reviewed the situation in detail. A check revealed that the ship had more ballast on board than the master had indicated, and it looked as if little or no ballast had been discharged during the attempt to refloat the ship the previous day. A further check showed nearly 21,000 tons on board. Steps were taken to see that no more misunderstandings would occur. The pumps were lined up, and it was decided to pump out all the ballast, except for No. 2 centre.

After helping the *Emsadler* to berth, the *Cycloop* returned and approached *Esso Peru* at 0930 on the 14th, and at 1009 the towing wire was fast. The ship commenced discharging ballast at full speed, and once this had been checked, the windlass was put in gear and the anchors, first one and then the other, were hove in.

At 1023 the ship's head started moving to port. At 1032 her position was checked, and it was found that she had moved about 100 feet.

At 1035, with the tug pulling at full power, the ship's engines were used to help break the hull suction.

At 1051 there were only 90 feet of chain out on each anchor, and engines were stopped as the chain was under the bow.

At 1055 both anchors were clear, and engines on half ahead, the ship began to move and her bows swung away from the reef towards deep water. From this point on, the engines were stopped and the *Cycloop* towed the *Peru* out into deep water and then up the eastern ship channel until eventually she was able to anchor at 1217 off the Brega Buoy.

The *Esso Peru* was subsequently towed to Malta for repairs, where she stayed for several weeks in drydock. Her bottom and rudder were extensively damaged. The fact that she survived after being driven over two reefs with little or no water over them, is a matter for wonder.

From a technical standpoint, the salvage of this vessel was not exceptional. The use of the anchors to assist the tug probably compensated for the lack of horsepower, but the major factor was starting to move the ship before the gale subsided and the water level dropped. The use of ballast to steady the vessel and reduce movement when she was aground was only practical on sand. It also helped to break the suction effect when pumped out in attempting to refloat the ship.

9 The grounding and salvage of the *Santa Kyriaki*

The salvage of the *Santa Kyriaki* is remarkable for two reasons. First, it involved the refloating of a lightly ballasted ship which had been driven ashore on a shallow sandy coast by a major gale, so that she was high and dry when the gale subsided. Secondly, on account of the equipment and manpower which was required between the 24th of November 1965, when the vessel grounded, and the 9th of March 1966 when the master signed the redelivery certificate in Amsterdam.

The vessel itself was rather old and small. Built in Scotland in 1945, her G.R.T. (gross registered tonnage) was 2925, S.D.W.T. 4570, length between perpendiculars 310 feet and she had a beam of 46 feet. A three island ship with two holds forward and one large one aft, she had a triple expansion engine and two Scotch boilers. Apart from a small emergency diesel generator, all her auxiliaries and deck machinery were powered by steam.

The actual grounding took place on the 24th of November, when she was approaching Ijmuiden on passage to Amsterdam in ballast.

A full gale was blowing from the north west with gusts at storm force and seas 10 to 12 feet high. The coastguard at Egmond first observed the vessel when she was $8\frac{1}{2}$ miles north of Ijmuiden Piers. As the *Santa Kyriaki* was dangerously close to shore they notified Bureau Wijsmuller at Ijmuiden, who despatched their tug *Titan*; but in view of the fact that no distress signal had been heard, and with the prevailing weather, the tug was ordered not to leave the shelter of the harbour entrance without something more definite.

The coastguard and the tug tried to contact the vessel without success, and the *Titan*, watching her on radar, saw the vessel heading for the entrance piers. She appeared to be out of control, and at 1220 reached a point 2 miles due south of Ijmuiden harbour entrance. Those on board the tug watched helplessly as, desperately, the master tried to swing back and head for the entrance, but his ship had insufficient power in ballast trim to get the bows right round and pointing north.

At about this time the vessel was observed to drop her starboard anchor. The cable parted almost immediately, and the port anchor was dropped soon after.

At 1230 the master of the *Titan* approached the stricken vessel as closely as possible, but could not get nearer than 2000 feet for fear of running aground. Meanwhile, the vessel itself had swung head to the wind and sea, and was gradually being driven further and further ashore. At 1245 the radio station at Bureau Wijsmuller's head office picked up the following radio message:

'Scheveningen Radio to *Santa Kyriaki* – Do you need assistance?'

'*Santa Kyriaki* to Scheveningen – With me tow, but as for you nil thank you.'

It was later established that *Santa Kyriaki* ran aground on the outer of three sandbanks at 1245. Thereafter the wind and breakers gradually forced her further ashore, and at 1305 it became clear that the *Titan* could not render any practical assistance, and was recalled to port.

At this stage it was difficult for all concerned to understand why the ship did not stand out to sea or ask the tug to take her in tow before she grounded. At the time the *Santa Kyriaki* was being driven up the beach, Bureau Wijsmuller were busy discovering who the vessel's agents were. At 1645 they sent a message via the ship's Ijmuiden agents, Messrs. Bebam, asking the vessel to fill up all double bottoms to avoid additional damage. At 1658 she replied that all tanks were full before the grounding.

Later a further message was sent asking the ship to flood the holds if she started pounding heavily. At 1805 the vessel replied that she was aground over her full length, and ballast had been put in Nos. 3 and 4 holds. Unfortunately, the wind had a major effect in increasing the height of the tide the day of the grounding. This undoubtedly caused the vessel to be driven ashore further than would have been the case with an ordinary rise of tide.

The next week was taken up with preparations for the salvage operation. On the 30th of November, the master of the *Santa Kyriaki* signed Lloyd's Open Form with N.V. Bureau Wijsmuller. Bureau Wijsmuller arranged for 75 gallons of fresh water and 50 gallons of fuel to be put on board for heating and cooking while all the salvage equipment was being prepared. Among the preparations required, Bureau Wijsmuller had to obtain permission from the authorities for the salvage. Permission was granted, but under several limiting conditions:

i)   The area in which sand could be removed and disposed of was restricted and carefully defined.

ii)   The area was to be fenced off and lighted with red lights at night, and warning notices for use in daylight.

iii) The beach was to be restored to its original condition, and all equipment removed after the salvage was completed.

The ship herself was found to be lying aground, heading 003°True, about 140 feet inshore of the low waterline, 220 feet from the dunes, and about 1·2 miles from the nearest paved access road. She had a 9 degree list to port and the starboard anchor and much of the chain was missing. The rudder was out of line, and the rudder post fractured.

All her double bottom tanks were full and the holds Nos. 1, 2 and 3 contained 40, 60 and 150 tons of water respectively. All her hatches were uncovered and covers stacked on deck. Apparently she had sailed without attempting to secure them. Her machinery appeared to be intact but a number of pipes leading to the ballast and general service pumps were fractured and the port boiler was operating, but at reduced temperature. A large scale soundings plan of the area was obtained to help plan the salvage operation.

The salvage plan

Initial efforts were aimed at preventing the ship from being driven any further up the beach. The first step called for the holds to be ballasted. In addition the port anchor and chain were to be kept tight, while the stern was secured by two ground tackles laid out aft to salvage anchors well offshore. The second step required a basin to be dug around the vessel using bulldozers and mobile sand suckers which had to be hired especially for the job. The idea was to lower the vessel bodily into this basin by washing the sand out from under the ship with high pressure water jets.

It was proposed, with the aid of the ground tackles and tugs towing on extra long wires, to turn the vessel onto an easterly heading and gradually work her seawards with this equipment, using tide and weather to the best advantage. It was calculated that the *Santa Kyriaki* could be refloated with a draft of 7 feet 4 inches forward and 10 feet 1 inch aft, and still retain a positive metacentric height of 8 feet 5 inches.

Enquiries were put in hand to locate and hire a small floating dredger to dig a channel for the ship to move seawards, but owners of such equipment were mostly unprepared to take the risk of letting their dredgers work in open sea, and those who were, demanded excessively high rates.

The first stage

Between the 3rd and 27th of December the time was taken up largely with logistic problems. The beach had to be fenced off to government requirements. Steel plates and other material had to be laid out over soft sand spots, to allow vehicles to pass from the access road to the vicinity of the ship. Water, oil and provisions had to be provided continuously to the ship for the master, chief and second engineers, wireless operator and cook, who remained on board, the rest of the crew having been taken off by helicopter. The weather did not help matters as between the 4th and 6th of December there was another gale which made work on the beach impossible. It was also getting much colder with the onset of winter.

A heavy lorry was used to transport big wires to the end of the access road. Each of these very long wires weighed about 6 tons. They consisted of:

One 6-inch wire – 2770 feet long
One 6-inch wire – 2000 feet long
One $5\frac{1}{4}$-inch wire – 2300 feet long
One $5\frac{1}{2}$-inch wire – 660 feet long

On board the ship preparation was made to repair the fractured pipes, and on the 3rd of December the port boiler had to be shut down as the forced draught fan broke down. On the 7th of December, when the wind and sea moderated, the first salvage equipment was hoisted on board using a Land Rover for power. It comprised two sets of ground tackle and a lot of ancillary equipment.

On the 8th of December, using the Land Rover and a double luff tackle, additional equipment was lifted on board. This included a diesel welding plant, one set of oxy-acetylene cutting equipment, three diesel pumps with bottles of gas, and numerous suction and delivery hoses. Additional salvage equipment was also taken on board to assist in rigging the ground tackles. Later in the day ten drums of gas oil were lifted on board for use with the diesel generator and the diesel pumps.

Nearly three tons of fresh water was pumped on board from a portable tank mounted on a truck which was hired for this purpose. On the 9th of December two of the big wires were transported from the point where they had been dumped to the ship, and then hauled on board using the heavy truck, though it had problems in the soft sand. On the 10th, three more heavy wires were brought to the ship and hauled on board in the same way. Work was also proceeding with the broken feed water pipes and boilers with a view to getting steam up. A diesel compressor was lifted on board with a view to using compressed air instead of steam to power one of the winches.

During the night a south west wind increased gradually to force 10 and the breakers crashing against the ship forced her further up the beach, at the same time listing her 14 degrees to port.

The 11th of December was spent rigging the ground tackles and securing them at the stern of the vessel, which involved cutting away some of the ship's rails, fitting rollers for the wires and reinforcing the bulkhead around the points where the ground tackles were anchored. This work continued for several days. At the same time marks were painted on the outside of the ship's hull, mainly along the port side, to measure the build-up of sand, as currents and tide appeared to be depositing sand along the port side.

On the 13th of December a decision was made to cut the rudder clear as it was useless, and several heavy wire strops were used to secure it prior to cutting it free. On the 14th, work commenced cutting through the stock and this was completed by the afternoon, but the heel was jammed and would not come clear of the sand. The sand had to be cleared while the tide was out.

On the 15th of December more of the stock was cut away and finally the rudder came clear, bringing with it 4 feet of the heel, which finally fractured. The work of supplying fresh water, stores and equipment went ahead steadily while the tackles were rigged and repairs continued in the boiler room.

Meanwhile preparations were going ahead to set the salvage anchors. The *Octopus* loaded these on the 15th, and on the 17th they were laid offshore in predetermined positions, accurately fixed by a special launch fitted with Decca. On the same day the tug *Hector*, working in conjunction with a shallow draft launch, attempted to pull a 2-inch wire rope out from the shore. Unfortunately, the manilla messenger rope broke.

On the 18th of December the welding and other ancillary work on the ship end of the ground tackles was completed, but the 19th proved to be unsuitable for an attempt to connect the ground tackle to the anchors, due to bad weather. On the 20th, the tug *Titan*, working with the shallow draft launch, managed to get the end of the 2-inch wire 3000 feet out to sea, where it was securely anchored and buoyed. The following day she passed the 2-inch wire to the *Octopus* and this vessel, which was anchored in deep water, managed to haul 1500 feet of 6-inch wire out from the ship. On the 22nd she secured the 6-inch wires to the two northern salvage anchors and commenced heaving a second 6-inch wire out from the *Santa Kyriaki*.

With temperature dropping and sleet and rain making the operation more difficult, 15 tons of gas oil was pumped aboard the ship from two tank trucks, on the 23rd of December. When loaded, these trucks had a tendency to sink in the sand, and frequently had to be assisted in getting out of soft sand areas.

In the engine room, work was progressing steadily. The ship's ballast pump was found to be beyond repair, and replaced by a 4-inch portable pump. Another 3-inch portable pump was connected up to No. 6 ballast tank to the cooling system, as all the intakes were blocked with sand or above water level. Nothing more could be done to connect the heavy wire to the southern salvage anchors, due to swell. Work on repairs continued on the 24th and 35 tons of gas oil was put on board from tank trucks. On the 27th of December the heavy wires were connected to the southern salvage anchors and the next day saw more pumps and equipment put aboard the *Santa Kyriaki*, together with 4 tons of water which was pumped on board. On the 30th of December the weather was bad, but a milestone was reached when the port boiler was fired up.

A portable diesel pump was used to clear the engine room of water, and No. 6 D.B. (double bottom) tank was opened to see if it could be used for feed water. The tank-bottom was set up, and some leaking rivets discovered. It was decided to use the tank for cooling water. During the afternoon the emergency diesel generator broke down and was replaced by a portable one. Three Wijsmuller men were used continuously to act as firemen, and to watch that the engine room equipment kept running properly. The major effort was to ensure that all heavy equipment, fuel and water were on board prior to the weather moderating, when work could start on digging a basin around the ship, prior to refloating her.

On the 3rd of January the weather improved sufficiently for work to start on excavating around the ship. The equipment used consisted of one dragline and shovel, one bulldozer, one pump and a powerful diesel for pumping sand and water. The work started with the digging of a trench along the length of the ship on the starboard (inshore) side. It had been noted that at high water the water level cut the ship's draft marks at 2 feet 8 inches forward, and 4 feet 8 inches aft.

On the 4th of January the dragline and shovel were brought into use, and by the end of the day a trench 12 feet deep had been cut along the inboard side of the ship, and sand started to crumble from under the ship. Work went on on board, pumping out holds and double bottoms and rigging the purchase gear for the southern ground tackle. On the 5th of January the new cooling system was finished, and a test run was tried on the main engine, but without success.

A test on empty double bottoms at high water indicated that Nos. 4 and 6 port tanks were leaking, as well as No. 5 starboard. When this was checked out beyond possibility of error, the sounding pipes and vents were plugged. It was calculated that if No. 1 D.B. tanks were filled, the vessel would have an even keel draft when she floated. These tanks had to be filled through the inspection hatches as the lines leading to No. 1 had leaks in Nos. 2 and 3 D.B. tanks, and the pipes had to be blanked off. In addition to the work on board, a high pressure pump was used to wash the sand away from under the ship on the starboard side while another trench was dug along the port side. This pump tended to run out of water at low tide, and as a result of trial and error it was found that flooding No. 2 hold during high water was the best way to keep it supplied for use when the tide receded.

The wind had gone to the east south east, and as a result the sea and swell were reduced, but it was also a lot colder and freezing at night. On the 6th and 7th work went on improving the basin, and washing the sand out from under the ship. On board, Wijsmuller engineers checked the crankshaft and found that the main crankshaft bearings were chafing against the cranks. Ingeniously they detached the main thrust block from its foundations and were able to shift the whole shaft aft about ⅜ of an inch. The thrust block was then resecured and the engine was ready for testing.

The 8th of January dawned with freezing conditions, but work went on day and night to make everything ready for high water on the 9th, when the spring tides would give enough water for a flotation attempt. Another big wire was successfully pulled out to deep water and buoyed by the *Titan*. By 1600 hours on the 9th all was ready, but the attempt was unsuccessful as the easterly winds cut the tides by more than 2 feet. An attempt to refloat on the 10th also had to be abandoned because of exceptionally low tides, but the ship's list decreased from 14 to 10 degrees. This list continued to decrease, and by the 13th was 2½ degrees. The digging and removal of sand, and other activities, were undertaken in unpleasant conditions, with sleet and snow and deck machinery freezing unless steam was left on deck.

Salvage crews are subjected to most of the environmental problems that other dangerous and exciting operations provide. At first, the excitement acts as a stimulant and motivates individuals in varying degrees. Experience has shown that this soon wears off. In the case of big ships loaded with valuable cargo, the salvage crew receive the additional buoyancy provided by the prospect of a large salvage award in which they will share. The peaks of optimism do not sustain the crews for too long, and if the particular job drags on, it can quite quickly give way to pessimism and a rapid deterioration of the alertness and efficiency, so badly needed in such work.

In the case of the *Santa Kyriaki* there was little to keep up the spirits of the salvage crew. The vessel was old and in ballast. At first the residents of houses nearby, and late visitors to the Dutch resorts in the vicinity, treated the beached vessel and the salvage crew to a great deal of interested curiosity. Several hundred walked across the sands during fine days and approached as near as the barriers would allow. Laughing and joking they pointed out the broken rudder and other items of interest to each other, and asked questions whenever one of the salvage crew strayed near them.

As the weather grew colder, fewer and fewer spectators came to look at the forlorn vessel sitting on the beach like a stranded whale, and as time moved on, her sides and begrimed appearance grew gradually worse. Rust streaked her ancient flanks and spread steadily to her upperworks and rigging. The cold east winds, sometimes at gale force, blew sand from the dunes against her sides and across her decks, whilst waves washed her hull and encrusted her with salt. For the Wijsmuller men, the problems were many and varied. Much of the work of digging and washing the sand out from under the ship was slow and heavy. At high water the sea undid much of the good work, and the operation had to be stopped, except at low water if the sea was at all rough.

Work continued in rain, snow and sleet. On board, working conditions were bad. In the engine room the poor light and badly maintained machinery provided headache after headache, and the boiler room was equally gloomy, the bulkheads coated with trickles of condensation – but at least it was warm.

For those who stayed on board, the restraints of living and working in a stranded ship without adequate heat and sanitary facilities, was something to be endured. At night, with freezing temperatures, it was necessary to keep steam on deck and to have all deck machinery actually in use turning over. A constant watch had to be kept to ensure that it did not stop and freeze up, otherwise fractured cylinders might put the winches out of action for good.

Those not on duty lay in musty cabins buried under piles of blankets, exhausted but subconsciously aware of the wheezing and rattling of the winches, and the echo of footsteps of those on duty as they clambered about the slippery decks. Living and working under such conditions can be depressing, and even dangerous for those concerned. It is necessary under such circumstances to watch the situation closely, and change the members of the salvage team when necessary.

The failure on the 9th meant that the vessel would not be refloated until the next spring tides, and the opportunity was taken to carry out a general reorganisation. Captain J. M. Birdie took over command of the operation, assisted by two engineers, and seven crew members from Wijsmuller. They lived on board continuously. Extra personnel worked on board on a day to day basis, and they and a small army of contract personnel, helped keep the vessel supplied with fresh water, oil and provisions. A V.H.F. radio was installed on board where contact could be maintained with the Wijsmuller office.

On the 22nd of January one of the firemen was injured by an explosion. He received bad burns to his right hand, but was able to put out the fire with an extinguisher, with the result that there was only minor damage.

During the period from the 23rd of January to the 1st of February, the work continued and good progress was made cutting the sand away from under the vessel and clearing the trench of sand and water with the pumps. The vessel was lowered considerably, and as the ground tackle was tightened, moved fractionally seaward. It had become apparent during these operations that the anchors securing the starboard ground tackle, were dragging. On the 1st of February the weather was fine, and the sea calm, so the *Octopus* was able to relay the southern set of anchors, and add an additional one to make sure they didn't drag. By heaving on the northern tackle only, the ship was turned slightly so that she was now heading 359°True.

In the engine room there were problems with the boilers, due to the lack of forced draught fan and the inability to repair it. On the 4th of February, during the p.m. high water, the tug *Gelderland* – 3000 h.p. – connected to one of the large wires offshore, but failed to move the vessel, due to a south wind which cut the height of the tide. The only notable thing that day was the forced draught fan which was finally repaired and tested successfully.

During the period 5th to 8th, southerly winds continued to cut predicted tidal heights, with the result that no serious attempt could be made to refloat the *Santa Kyriaki*, and the prospects of floating her before the spring tides in March, receded. It was decided to build a 4-foot dyke of sand around the basin, and to provide a gap which could be closed at high water or just after the tide started to drop. In this way the basin would retain much of the water brought in by the tide, and once the gap was closed, high capacity pumps could create an artificially high water level in the basin which would permit the ship to be swung, or even refloated.

During the evening of the 8th, the fan motor lubricating system failed, causing the bearings to run hot, with the result that the fan had to be stopped, dismantled and sent ashore for repair. It was not returned until the next day. Work building the 4-foot dyke and supplying the ship with water, fuel and provisions went on, hampered by the cold weather, during which freezing conditions meant that salt had to be spread over the deck, and steam maintained on deck machinery on a twenty four hour basis.

On the 11th of February a high capacity pump was brought into service. This was a screw pump with a capacity of 1400 tons per hour and was operated with a power take off from a large tractor.

On the 13th and 14th there were heavy falls of snow which made conditions on the shore even more difficult, and the quantity of fresh water required to maintain steam and other essential services, increased.

On the 16th of February, a second screw pump was brought into service with the object of making an attempt to float the vessel in the basin on the 17th, during the morning tide. This attempt was duly made, but failed to move her. With the appalling weather conditions the failure of this attempt caused considerable disappointment and conjecture as to whether it was possible to salvage the ship without the use of a dredger. Finally, it was decided to make an all out effort to obtain a small dredger.

Work on the beach was stopped temporarily during the period 18th to 26th of February, but during high water periods the ground tackle was tightened, and on a number of occasions the vessel became lively, but without moving significantly.

On the 27th, a hire agreement for a small dredger was concluded and it was delivered to the site on the 28th by a heavy truck. A considerable amount of preparation had to be done to provide a surface on the beach for the truck to approach the ship. Plates were laid over soft spots, and a bulldozer was used to help compact the sand.

The dredger consisted of a powerful pump powered by a diesel engine mounted on floats and a suction pipe suspended from a small gantry, which allowed it to be lifted out of the way or moved from one point to another on a limited arc. The weather was too rough to start dredging, but the time was used to lay the delivery pipe from the dredger to a point north west of the *Santa Kyriaki*, which had been designated as a shoal area. During the evening the wind dropped sufficiently to allow the dredger to be positioned, and at 2215 it commenced work.

The plan now was for the dredger to dredge a basin for itself to float at all states of the tide. Once this had been done it commenced excavating a trench all along the port side of the ship, gradually deepening it to allow the sand to run down from under the ship. Apart from occasions when the suction clogged, good progress was made, and the ship sank slowly, but noticeably lower. The only breaks in dredging were caused by blocked suctions or waves at or near high water.

On the 4th of March the *Octopus* relaid the three anchors of the south ground tackle as they still had a tendency to come home. Dredging was also concentrated around the stern. The following day, during the p.m. high water, the weight was taken on the ground tackles and the ship's engines were put astern. As a result the stern moved 65 feet seaward and the ship's head swung to 030°True, marking the most significant progress to date.

On the 6th of March another maximum effort was made. During the low water period the dredger enlarged the basin around the stern, and prior to high water the *Titan* picked up the towing wire offshore. During a $2\frac{1}{2}$-hour period covering high tide, the strain was taken on the ground tackles and the tug sheered back and forth on the towing wire.

As the depth of water increased, the vessel began to move and with the ship's engine, used alternatively ahead and astern, she was gradually swung so that the stern moved seaward, and the ship's head changed to 068°True. Unfortunately, the suction pipe of the dredger was blocked by an old anti-tank mine, and the area had to be cleared until a mine disposal squad had removed it.

On the 7th of March further progress was made. At low water a bulldozer was used to cut into the inner of the three sand bars, while the dredger continued to enlarge the basin on the port side and around the stern of the ship. The *Titan*, assisted by the tug *Simson* resumed towing. As high water approached, the weight was put on the ground tackle, and the engine used in short bursts ahead and astern. The ship's stern moved seaward, and the vessel's head changed to 118°True. This time the swell and weight imposed fractured the cheek of the starboard winch, and the repair job necessitated all night work in the Wijsmuller workshops to have it ready for the next day.

On the 8th, the winch was damaged beyond repair when the drive gear shattered. This meant rerigging the purchase wire to the winch on the forecastle using two snatch blocks, and burning two holes in the superstructure, which had to be done by high water – predicted for 1650 hours. During the high water period the ship was moved 120 feet seaward, using the ground tackles, and the tugs *Simson* and *Titan*.

As the tide started to recede, a race against time started as it was felt she could be refloated. The carpenter's stoppers were resecured, and the strain taken once again. Meanwhile, the ship's sole remaining anchor and chain was slipped and buoyed.

Just after 1700 hours the *Santa Kyriaki* finally slid off the last bank, and *Titan* towed her clear of the shallows. During the same evening the ship was towed into Ijmuiden, and eventually delivered to her owners at the Amsterdam Drydock Company.

The salvage operation was still not complete. Even after the vessel was redelivered, the rudder and anchor and chain had to be collected and the salvage equipment removed, and it took a further two weeks to restore the beach to the satisfaction of the authorities.

In reviewing this operation, the supply problem stands out as a major hurdle. A total of 180 tons of gas oil and 1800 tons of fresh water were put on board the ship while she was aground.

10 The salvage of the Italian tanker *Mare Nostrum*

The *Mare Nostrum* stranded on the 18th of September 1966 at 2155 hours while proceeding at full speed. The ship was in ballast bound for Mena al Ahamadi from Naples, and grounded on Hallaniya Island, giving her position as 17° 27′ North, 56° 14′ East when sending out the customary distress message by radio.

The news that the *Mare Nostrum* had gone aground on an island off the coast of Arabia reached the Wijsmuller head office in Ijmuiden at 0136 on the 19th of September, but there was some confusion as to where the vessel had gone aground as the telex message received in Ijmuiden gave the position incorrectly as 27° North, 56° 14′ East – the correct latitude being 17° 27′ North. Unaware of this, Wijsmuller's sent a telex to their tug *Friesland* on station at Daiyer in the Persian Gulf, to proceed to the assistance of the ship which was estimated to have stranded about 280 miles from the *Friesland*.

Meanwhile, a telex was sent to the owners of *Mare Nostrum* – Compagnie d'Armamento in Rome – offering the services of the *Friesland* on the basis of Lloyd's Salvage Agreement, 'No Cure – No Pay'. At 0828 on the 19th, a telex was received from the ship's agents in Genoa giving the correct position, and at 0830 the *Friesland* was given the new information. Even though it meant she would have to steam 980 miles instead of 280, the tug was instructed to proceed.

On the 20th of September, Lloyds informed Bureau Wijsmuller that the British motor tanker *Pearleaf* had taken on board the entire crew of forty men, and that the stranded ship had been abandoned. The following day the tug managed to contact the *Pearleaf* by radio, and was informed by the master of the *Mare Nostrum* that all her tanks were leaking and in his opinion the vessel could not be salved.

It was decided in Ijmuiden to await the report of the master of the *Friesland* before making any decision, and as she was due at the scene of the casualty at 1700 hours on the 22nd, there was not too long to wait. In fact, he delayed his inspection till daylight on the 23rd. This was a wise decision as the vessel was stranded in

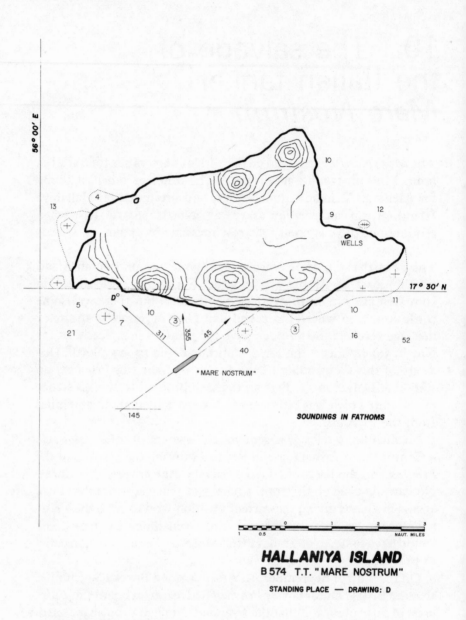

SOUNDINGS IN FATHOMS

HALLANIYA ISLAND
B 574 T.T. "MARE NOSTRUM"
STANDING PLACE — DRAWING: D

a location which was poorly surveyed and charted, and made hazardous by an outlying reef.

At 1500 on 23rd, the *Friesland* passed the preliminary report to Ijmuiden stating that the ship had gone aground on hard rocks, and as far as could be seen no damage had been sustained above the water line. The engine room and main cargo pumproom were dry and all cargo tanks except Nos. 4, 8 and 10 starboard, were tidal.

This preliminary report was considered in Ijmuiden as significant. It was decided that as the vessel was a conventional twin longitudinal bulkhead vessel with thirty cargo tanks and undamaged pumproom and engine room, it might be possible to refloat the ship using compressed air. Accordingly it was decided to send experts to investigate whether the salvage was really possible.

Two experts, Messrs. Gatersleben and de Nobel, left Amsterdam for Aden on the 24th of September, and arrived at 0600 the next day. With the assistance of the local agent, the two Wijsmuller men inspected the repair facilities at Aden with a view to seeing what salvage equipment was available for hire in the port, and to establish if the port could do any repairs to the ship. They found that there was ample equipment available for hire, such as compressors and generators, but the dockyard was limited to hull and engine repairs and could not drydock the ship.

The agent was able to arrange a meeting with the representative of the owner's insurance company and the captain, who had been landed by the *Pearleaf* at Bahrein, and flown to Aden. This meeting proved useful as considerable additional information was made available to the Wijsmuller experts.

The captain indicated that the ship had a draft of 17 feet 3 inches forward, 24 feet 9 inches aft, and had 11,130 tons of ballast on board at the time she went aground. He provided the Wijsmuller men with soundings taken round the ship and the ullages of all the tanks.

In the discussion that followed, he revealed the fact that after stranding, he had tried to pump out the leaking tanks with the ship's cargo pumps without success. He put the failure down to broken suction pipes in the tanks, as well as broken valve spindles. His plan showed that only Nos. 4, 6 and 9 starboard wing tanks were undamaged, and the forepeak, cofferdam and forward pumproom were flooded.

A review of the ship's machinery revealed that she was propelled by General Electric steam turbine developing 16,000 s.h.p. The steam was generated by two water tube boilers, and a Sulzer diesel generator and various other steam and electrically driven pumps and auxiliaries were fitted including five compressors. All of this equipment had been shut down and left in working condition when the ship was abandoned. As a result of the talks with the agents, it was decided to fly to Mukalla where the *Friesland* would meet them.

The 27th of September was spent getting visas and trying to arrange, through the agents and with the British Authorities,

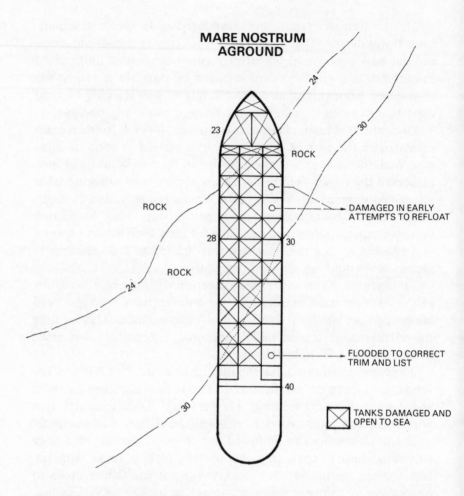

MARE NOSTRUM AGROUND

for some guards to be placed on the *Mare Nostrum* in view of the political situation and risk to the salvage crew from terrorists operating in and around the Aden Protectorate and Sheikdom of Oman.

At 0800 on the 28th, the two Wijsmuller salvage experts accompanied by the ship's master and Mr. Blandini, the owner's insurance representative, left Aden Airport for Mukalla. The party landed at Ryan Airport, near Mukalla, and were met by the local agent. Formalities included a visit to the British High Commissioner and R.A.F. authorities, after which the group waited at the local hotel for the arrival of the *Friesland*. Mukalla proved to be a very small port with no possibility of providing any equipment or technical assistance which might be needed to assist with the salvage.

The tug arrived during the early hours of the 29th of September and the party of four boarded her just before nine as she lay at anchor. Prior to sailing, Mr. Blandini talked to the master of the *Friesland*, and then announced he was returning to Aden as he was now convinced the *Mare Nostrum* was a constructive total loss. He then disembarked and the tug weighed anchor and sailed at 0925.

During the forty-hour passage from Mukalla to the scene of the stranding, the master of the ship provided the two salvage inspectors with the detailed information which his inspection had revealed. He had taken soundings all round the vessel and observed the draft marks at high water when the level reached 22 feet forward, 24 feet amidships and 27 feet aft. At high water she was nearly upright, but as the tide fell, developed a list of about 5 degrees to port. The master of the tug stated that the ship was hard aground on the rocks with extensive bottom damage, and there was insufficient buoyancy to give her any movement even at high water. His inspection of the ship revealed that the afterpeak was dry, and that the double bottoms under the engine room, the after cofferdam and the main cargo pumproom, had not been damaged and had developed no leaks. He had also taken ullages of the cargo tanks, and this revealed that Nos. 4, 6, 8, 9 starboard and No. 7 port appeared to be relatively watertight and had not flooded to the same extent as most of the other tanks, which had ullages varying from 21 to 28 feet.

The fact that there might be one good tank on the port side was encouraging, but the master stressed that inspection through open tank coamings indicated that there was a lot of damage in the cargo tanks. Torn plates could be heard to grind together and there was considerable evidence of damage to bulkheads and cargo piping.

As can be expected, at the end of September, the south west monsoon was fitful and had started to blow itself out, and the wind and sea were slight, which allowed the *Friesland* to make her full speed arriving off Hallaniya Island in the early hours of the 1st of October.

Standing off at a short distant, the tug's searchlight was played over the wreck and it was observed that there were five or six people on board. There was no response to attempts to communicate by signal lamp, except that the people on board displayed a steady white light. In view of the warnings they had been given about terrorists, it was decided to stand clear till daylight. At 0630 the motor boat was lowered and the two salvage experts, and several officers and crew members set out for the wreck.

Prior to boarding, the motor boat was used to carry out an inspection by going around the wreck slowly. Both anchors were in the hawse pipes and the two after lifeboats were missing, the falls hanging in the water. It then became apparent that the people on board were British soldiers protecting the wreck, so at 0710 the party boarded the ship via a pilot ladder which had been lowered over the port side.

There were five British soldiers on board and the officer in charge indicated that he and his men had been landed from L.C.T. *Agheila*, which had been passing on an inspection of the coast. While in the vicinity of the *Mare Nostrum*, a dhow had been seen close to the wreck, but it had made off at its best speed and threading its way between the reefs to discourage pursuit. The commander of the *Agheila* had sent off an inspection party, and had left some men on board to prevent further plundering. The L.C.T. was due back in two days. Inspection of the ship revealed that she had been plundered, and that raiders had caused considerable damage, and obviously been in the act of removing a large number of tools and equipment when they had been interrupted.

Messrs. Gatersleben and de Nobel carried out a detailed inspection of the ship, assisted by the boarding party from the tug. The looters had unbolted the radar and gyro compass and had stacked tools and other equipment ready for removal, but they had not touched any of the compressors and other equipment vital for the salvage operation.

Inspection of the engine room revealed that leakage from the stern gland and other sources had allowed a great deal of water to accumulate in the engine room bilges. In addition, the poor ventilation and change of temperature from night to day had created a condensation problem which over twelve days had an adverse effect on all electrical equipment, such as switchboards, electric motors, etc. Before anything else was done it would be necessary to pump out the bilges in the engine room and boiler room, and dry out the electrical equipment by improving the ventilation.

A check on the soundings around the ship confirmed the master's first report. The ship was aground for her full length from forward up to an area in the vicinity of Nos. 6 and 7 cargo tanks on the port side, but it was apparent that she had run ashore at an angle to the ridge of rocks, as on the port side she was aground to an area in the vicinity of No. 2 and 3 starboard. This accounted for the reports that a number of starboard wing tanks were intact. A check showed that only Nos. 4, 6, 8, 9 and 10 starboard wing tanks were tight. The vital No. 7 port was tidal and so was No. 7 centre, which had suffered bottom damage with all the others.

There was a swell of approximately 8 feet which did not move the ship, but the tidal range which was about 3 feet caused her to list about $4\frac{1}{2}$ degrees to port at low water, and to straighten about 2 degrees at high water. After reviewing the situation, the two salvage inspectors were of the opinion that the *Mare Nostrum* could be refloated. The hull still had sufficient strength to take the strain of refloating and the tow to a repair port. This opinion was made known to Bureau Wijsmuller by radio telephone from the *Friesland* with a request for a salvage team to be flown out to assist with the work. It was felt that at least five men would be required, and Ijmuiden agreed to send two engineers with experience of salvage work, two divers and a carpenter. As a result of this radio telephone call, Bureau Wijsmuller got in touch with the underwriters, with whom a limited contract had been signed on the 23rd of September to cover the work done by the tug, and the inspection. As a result of the favourable report by the Wijsmuller experts a new contract was concluded, signed and back dated to cover the work already done.

It was anticipated that two or three weeks' work would be required prior to any attempt to refloat the ship. There were a number of problems which had to be solved, not the least of which was manpower. The tug was supplying this requirement, but it was causing problems because it could not anchor safely, as the water was too deep off the reef and no safe anchorage could be found within easy steaming range. Consequently, the crew had to keep watches as the tug steamed around in the vicinity. The situation was made worse because, as night fell, the dying monsoon frequently freshened from the south west sometimes blowing as hard as force 7 or 8, and causing a nasty sea. In such conditions there were limits to the tug's capacity to provide manpower and assistance with boats and equipment.

In spite of the problems, work was started and steady progress was made. Among the first steps taken was the transhipment of a portable diesel generator with cables and lighting equipment, together with tools and two compressed air bottles from the *Friesland* to the *Mare Nostrum*.

With the portable diesel generator it was possible to provide limited domestic and engine room lighting, and by opening the skylights, and training ventilators on the wind, the circulation of air in the engine room was improved. With better lighting and ventilation in the engine room, Mr. de Nobel started work on the diesel generator. With the aid of a compressed air bottle he got the diesel engine going, and after checking and cleaning the circuits and switchboard, managed to start an electric bilge pump with which the water in the engine room and boiler room was pumped overboard.

On the 2nd of October the *Friesland* made radio contact with *Agheila* and was advised that she would be in the vicinity of the wreck the following day. Arrangements were made for the Commander of the L.C.T. to discuss the situation with the Wijsmuller salvage inspectors when the vessel arrived.

Meanwhile, with the assistance of the master of the *Mare Nostrum*, a number of jobs were started. The radar and gyro compass were restored to their proper positions on the bridge, but could not be tested. The magnetic compass was also replaced and showed the ship to be heading 047° True. On the main deck all the tanks were opened, and each carefully checked with a detector to make sure that there was no gas present. Work was also started on making the deck fittings airtight. Each Butterworth plate was inspected and, where necessary, packing, bolts and nuts were renewed.

In the engine room the work continued. The ship's diesel generator was overheating due to a malfunction of the cooling system, so it had to be stopped for overhaul, and work was started on the ship's compressors with a view to getting them operational as soon as possible.

On the 3rd of October work continued as outlined, but at 1600 hours was interrupted by the arrival of the *Agheila* in the vicinity. A meeting with her captain resulted in an agreement to leave three armed soldiers to protect the salvage workers, on the understanding that the salvage crew would feed the men and convey them to Aden at Bureau Wijsmuller's expense. Before departing the captain of the L.C.T. indicated that he would be back in the area about the 14th of October.

On the 4th of October, work on the Butterworth openings into the cargo tanks was completed. Work was now started on sealing the cargo tank venting system. Each gas line was sealed by plugging the openings into the individual tank coamings with wooden plugs and rubber packing, and in some cases by removing the valves from the vent lines and blanking the tanks off. The stranded ship was 12 years old, and this work was made more difficult by a certain amount of corrosion in the material of which the pipes and valves

were constructed. In the engine room, the malfunction in the auxiliary diesels' cooling system had been fixed and was once again in
use. Examination of the ship's compressors had revealed that
though all were capable of running, they were in a poor state of
maintenance and spares would have to be ordered and installed
before the compressors could be used continuously to keep the ship
afloat.

Messages were sent via the *Friesland* to Ijmuiden listing the parts
required. A lightweight gas turbine compressor with all the necessary hoses etc. was also requested as a precaution and back up,
the plan being that the five-man salvage team would bring the
equipment with them. Meanwhile, the tug's motor boat tran-
shipped three portable diesel pumps, together with suction and discharge hoses and sufficient fuel to last two days. In addition, a 5½-
inch steel wire rope 325 feet long was brought over and secured
to the bitts aft, and rigged so that it led through a panama lead
right aft, and then secured in bights along the starboard side where
it was ready for instant use and could be made available for towing
by cutting the lashing.

On the 5th of October the swell, which had been from the
south west previously, changed direction gradually till it was coming almost from the south east. About 7 feet high, it started breaking on the starboard side of the ship, making her work and roll.
Using the portable diesel pumps, No. 9 starboard was filled to ease
the vessel's movement, but it also served as a means of testing the
watertight condition of the tank. As it was not possible to move
the weight from the starboard side, the water was then transferred
to No. 8 starboard, by lowering the actual pump into No. 9 starboard as the water level fell, and using two pumps in series to overcome the static head. In this way the watertight integrity of all the
tanks was checked over the next few days and the sound ones could
be pumped dry.

On the 6th of October, the weather improved and the swell
reduced. As well as testing tanks, work was started on sealing the
ventilators and manhole doors into the forepeak, forward cofferdams and transfer pumproom. The tank lids on all the tanks to
be filled with compressed air were inspected, packing renewed
where necessary, then coated with sealing compound and screwed
up tight. In many cases the packing on valve spindles had to be
renewed and the glands screwed up to prevent the air from leaking
out through these openings. Another source of air leakage was the
mountings on each tank containing the tapes for the automatic

ullage system. In most cases these had to be blanked off, but on a number of these, mountings were used to fit air gauges to measure the air pressure in the tanks. In the engine room a test run was conducted on the main compressors, all of which were operated but found to be in need of considerable maintenance.

Inspector B. Gatersleben now began to consider when the first attempt to refloat the *Mare Nostrum* should be made. The highest tides were predicted for the 13th and 14th of October, and he decided that if everything was ready the best chance lay on either of these two days, so Ijmuiden was informed accordingly.

On the 7th a new manifold, made on the *Friesland* and fitted with adaptors to take the air hoses, was connected to the ship's cargo tank smothering system. Test runs pumping air into Nos. 8, 9 and 10 port revealed many leaks in the smothering system and other odd locations on deck. These leaks had to be fixed with various materials, such as VECOM E-12 liquid iron, and glass cloth patches covered with protective canvas bandages. By 2300 hours the three tanks were tight, and work started on the other tanks which were to be used for compressed air.

Tanks 4, 6, 7, 8 and 10 starboard had all been pumped dry using the *Friesland*'s portable pumps in series. This operation required the pump operator to enter the tank using breathing apparatus. Tanks 1, 5 and 9 starboard, though tight, remained full to keep the vessel upright.

On Saturday the 8th of October the weather was fine with light southerly breezes, clear sky and a low swell. Work continued on making the port wing tanks airtight at deck level, and by 1800 hours this had been completed. In the engine room the third of the ship's compressors was given a trial run after a successful overhaul. The motor boat was kept busy transporting fuel for the pumps and generators, and a spare portable radio to permit voice contact between the two ships was now brought over from the *Friesland*. This proved to be a great help, and one of the first messages relayed to the *Mare Nostrum* indicated that the salvage team and the spares and other equipment ordered, had arrived at Aden.

There was a hold up in obtaining visas, and in attempting to get the party flown to Salalah. On the 9th, time was spent in fitting extra pressure gauges to provide pressure readings in the tanks, as well as on the service lines being used. In the engine room work started on the two small compressors used in conjunction with the ship's cold stores and freezer room. The intention was to adapt them to help with providing air for the cargo tanks, as once the vessel was afloat she would depend entirely on the air supply to stop her listing to port and even sinking.

On the 10th of October, work continued plugging leaks and making ready for the first attempt to refloat the ship. Two inflatable dinghies were brought over from the *Friesland* for safety purposes, as well as welding and cutting gear. At 2130 a message was received from Aden to say that the salvage party had been delayed still further. Visas to get the party by air to Salalah were unobtainable and no suitable vessel had been found as yet to bring them out to the *Mare Nostrum*.

Inspector Gatersleben decided that though he really had insufficient men on board to handle an emergency during refloating, they needed to use the bigger tides to get the ship off, and therefore must start at once to refloat her, as it would take forty eight hours to deballast and press up the tanks with compressed air. Ijmuiden were informed of the change of plan, and work started on deballasting and rigging flexible hoses so that the two small compressors could be hooked into the system.

On the 11th of October work continued. The tug connected up ready for towing, and lay off, putting sufficient weight on the wire to stop it fouling the propeller. At high water, which occurred at 1915, she towed at full power for approximately two hours without the ship moving. The only result was an increase in the list to $7\frac{1}{2}$ degrees. A message was received via the *Friesland* that the salvage party would be arriving on the 13th in the Swedish *Pearl Sea*, and arrangements were made to transfer them and their equipment with the tug's motor boat.

On the 12th of October work went on with deballasting the starboard tanks and pressurising the centre and port tanks. Air leaks occurred frequently and were dealt with immediately. At 0730 hours another attempt was made to tow her off, but with no success, though the port list increased to 9 degrees. The pressure inside the tanks was maintained at about 5 lb. per square inch, and it was calculated that this displaced the water in the tanks about 16 feet below normal sea level outside, with a corresponding increase in buoyancy.

The 9 degrees port list meant that had the ship been afloat she would have been drawing considerably more water on the port side than the starboard side, and as she was aground the list was obviously not helping.

Soundings taken at 1600 hours around the vessel showed the following depths:

	Port side	*Starboard side*
Off the bow	23 feet	24 feet
Level with the bridge	28 feet 3 inches	30 feet
Break of the poop	30 feet	40 feet.

After considering the situation, it was decided to fill No. 10 starboard wing tank, as this would help to reduce the port list and increase the trim by the stern, thereby lifting her forward. While No. 10 was being filled the *Friesland* had another attempt on the evening tide to pull the ship off. This attempt also failed. On the 13th of October at 0600 hours, No. 10 starboard was full and the vessel was definitely trimmed more by the stern. As high water approached, the list improved and the tug commenced towing at full power and sheering to try to get the *Mare Nostrum* moving.

At 0845 the ship's head altered slightly and the list had reduced to 2 degrees, but this attempt also failed to refloat her, and as the tide fell the list increased, and the head swung back to within 1 degree of its original direction. Inspection along the port side showed shell plating protruding from the bottom of Nos. 7 and 8 port. Nos. 2 and 3 starboard, which had previously been watertight, were now leaking and had to be made tight and rigged for compressed air.

The next attempt was made on the evening tide. By 1830, No. 2 and 3 starboard were tight, and these tanks were pressurised at once. At the same time No. 1 starboard, which was tight and full of ballast, was discharged overboard to increase the lift forward. At 2100 hours the ship's head began to move again, and this time did not return to the original heading at low water. The *Friesland* kept a steady strain on the ship all the time using less than half power. At 0001 on the 14th of October, those on board the ship could feel movement. She appeared to be pivoting about a central point in way of No. 2 centre tank, and the heading slowly changed to 028°True.

At 0130 Inspector Gatersleben was convinced that the ship had moved astern. To assist the lift forward he ordered the pressurisation of all tanks aft of the bridge to be stopped, and increased the pressure in Nos. 1 and 4 port and centre tanks, and Nos. 2 and 3 starboard, while still continuing to deballast No. 1 starboard. The intense noise of working and grinding metal in No. 2 centre made it appear that plating protruding from the bottom in this area was stopping the vessel refloating. By 0300 the vessel's head had swung to due North, and at 0500 the noise of grinding stopped as she appeared to come free. At 0515 the ship's head was 330° True, but as there were no shore lights the position of the ship could not be verified. Shortly afterwards, the master of the *Friesland*, which had been towing at full power, confirmed that the *Mare Nostrum* was afloat, and that the shore line was receding very slowly on his radar.

While the tug was assisting the refloating, its motor boat had taken the salvage party from *Pearl Sea* with their equipment and transferred them back to the *Friesland*. There were only thirteen men on the ship when it was refloated, three of whom were British soldiers.

The *Friesland* towed the ship slowly away from the land until it was about ½ mile off, where the motor boat was able to transfer the salvage team and their equipment. Once the men and equipment were on board, the ship was towed stern first until the two were about 10 miles from the nearest land. At about 1700 hours towing was stopped, and the wire pennant was let go on the stern of the *Mare Nostrum*. After recovering the towing gear, the *Friesland* made fast to the ship forward, and by 1930 tug and tow were ready to start the voyage to Aden.

While under tow the *Mare Nostrum* lay quietly with a slight list to port, lifting gently to a long low swell which came from the east. The reinforcements and their equipment helped considerably. One of the first steps taken was to fit a pressure regulator on the main air supply line. In this way the air pressure and output of the compressors could be controlled fairly easily. The low pressure gas turbine compressor was made operational and connected into the system. As soon as these jobs had been done, a complete inspection of the ship was carried out without finding any major leakage or problems, but the compressors were kept going maintaining 0.4 of an atmosphere above normal atmospheric pressure. The system was inspected regularly in case of leaks or failure of equipment.

Navigation lights were displayed and the *Friesland* indicated that the tow was making about 2 knots. On Saturday the 15th of October a comprehensive inspection of the cargo and other tanks was started. All the starboard cargo wing tanks, with the exception of Nos. 2 and 3, which were damaged during refloating, were watertight. In addition, the after pumproom cofferdam and bunker tanks, as well as the boiler and engine room, had suffered no damage. A proper check on the double bottom tanks in the engine room and the afterpeak, also showed these to be watertight. The inspection confirmed that all the other compartments, including No. 10 port and centre cargo tanks were tidal, and that this also applied

to the forepeak, forward bunker tanks, as well as the forward cofferdam and transfer pumproom.

The real question was, how bad was the bottom damage? The
low speed the tow was making indicated that some of the bottom
plating was hanging down and creating a drag. To get a feel for
the extent of the damage, each of the cargo tanks was isolated in
turn, depressurised and inspected by divers using safety lines. The
clear water and sunlight from outside showed clearly how much
bottom plating was missing, and in the case of No. 10 port a large
section was hanging down under the ship. All the port tanks were
inspected on the 15th of October, and the centre tanks the following
day.

While this work was in progress the pressure relief valves which
were leaking, were made airtight to reduce the loss of air. The starboard cargo tanks were pumped dry except for Nos. 5 and 10 which
were kept full to prevent the ship listing to port. The portable gas
turbine was given a test run. By the 17th of October the air leakage
had been reduced to minor proportions and it was decided to dis-
continue the use of the compressors except to recharge the system.

There was now time to turn to other things. The meat and store
rooms had to be cleared of their rotting contents and the vermin
they had attracted. The smell was terrible and all of it was dumped
overboard and the interior of the store rooms washed out. Living
accommodation was also cleaned up and essential repairs made to
damaged doors etc. which had been smashed in by the looters. The
L.C.T. *Agheila* was in radio contact with the *Friesland* and indicated she had a compressor on board for the ship which had been
hired from the Aden Drydock Company. It was estimated that the
L.C.T. would be in the vicinity of the tow at 0200 on the 18th,
and would tranship the compressor and stores if the weather permitted.

The tug was also in contact with Ijmuiden and passed on
messages concerning the bottom damage. As a result of this
exchange of messages, Ijmuiden asked to talk to Inspector Gatersleben, and he was transferred to the *Friesland* by the motor boat.
During this conversation the condition of the ship's bottom plating
was discussed and the fact that a large section was hanging under
the ship increasing the draft as much as 30 feet and slowing her
progress. This was considered both from the standpoint of temporary repairs and improvements when the ship reached Aden, but
also what would need to be done there before permission could
be given to pass through the Suez Canal. It was agreed to send

underwater cutting gear and another diver to Aden, and a quantity of other vital equipment was also ordered.

On Tuesday the 18th of October, contact was made with the *Agheila* at about 0130. At approximately 0300 she went alongside the tug and transferred some stores, then at 0335 came alongside the *Mare Nostrum* on the starboard side. Two of the three soldiers then returned to the L.C.T., while one remained on board on the understanding that he would be landed at Aden, where he was needed.

The transfer of the compressor proved a problem. It was lifted off the deck of the *Agheila*, but as it was suspended from a davit on a double luff tackle it could not be lifted high enough to clear the side. The L.C.T. left with the compressor secured, still hanging over the side, and it was not until later, and with the assistance of more tackle obtained from *Friesland*, that it was finally swung inboard. Some damage was sustained which was later repaired on board.

From time to time it was necessary to start the compressors and renew the air pressure on the cargo tanks. On a number of occasions one or other of the ship's compressors became unserviceable and had to be repaired, but at no time did the supply of air drop to the extent that it caused anxiety. From the 19th to the 22nd of October work continued cleaning the ship up and restoring defective machinery. A refrigerator in the galley was repaired and started successfully, but progress was very slow.

On the 23rd of October the distance to Aden was 330 miles, which meant another seven days at 2 knots, and various ways of increasing the speed were discussed. It was decided that the best solution probably lay in getting the vessel's propulsion plant operating, and a start was made with a view to seeing if one of the boilers could be flashed up. An inspection of both boilers and the ancillary equipment, such as feed and fuel pumps as well as forced draught ventilation and fans, indicated that it was practical to raise steam, and the port boiler was chosen for the initial attempt after the tubes and furnaces had been looked at. The super heat tubes had to be drained of water and dried out. The heavy fuel had solidified in the fuel lines and it was necessary to heat the fuel with steam before it could be passed through the piping to the fuel pump and then to the burners in the furnaces.

The sudden shut down of the boilers had left the burners and the boiler combustion chambers heavily coked with carbonised oil. All of this equipment had to be cleaned and the blocked pipes cleared with compressed air before a start could be made getting steam up. It would also be necessary to use some of the limited supply of gas oil to fire the boiler initially, so that steam could be produced to heat the heavy fuel in the bunker tanks. Other difficulties were experienced, such as the inability of the diesel auxiliary generator to produce enough power to run the forced draught fans and pumps necessary to start up the boiler. One by one, each of the difficulties was overcome. After draining the tubes and cleaning out the furnaces, the boiler was filled with distilled water from the reserve tank by using the auxiliary boiler water feed pump. Windsails were rigged to improve the natural draught, and by late afternoon on the 23rd the port boiler was fired and gradually steam was circulated to warm the boiler through and remove water from the system. At 2100 the port boiler registered a pressure of 3k/cm^2. After further testing and heating it was raised to 10k/cm^2 and then 20k/cm^2, or half the designed operating pressure.

While work was going ahead on the port boiler, a constant watch was kept on the cargo tanks, and steps were taken to strengthen the forward bulkhead in the main pumproom by shoring it up with timber and flooding the cofferdams aft of No. 10 wings. On the 24th of October, sufficient steam was available to allow the main steam generator to be started, which allowed full use of the electrical feed and fuel pumps as well as the forced draught fans, and after a time to warm the main turbine through. At 1130 the turbine was started and the speed increased gradually. The *Mare Nostrum*'s steering gear had to be brought into operation as the vessel was now sheering heavily.

With steam available, other jobs were started. The ship's galley was made operational and the after accommodation was cleaned, a start was made to clean the midship accommodation. In addition, two derricks were topped and the compressor hired from the Aden Drydock Company was moved to a better position. The ship was now making about 3.5 knots, and by 2100 hours this was increased to 4 knots. The 26th of October was spent in getting the vessel shipshape for arrival at Aden. Doors were secured, mooring ropes brought up onto the forecastle and poop. Portholes were closed to prevent pilfering.

On the 27th the tow arrived off the port, and with the assistance of two harbour tugs and a pilot, entered the harbour. The ship was swung with great difficulty due to the plates fouling the muddy bottom, and at 2015 was securely tied up to a set of mooring buoys. At this point the salvage operation was really concluded as the *Mare*

Nostrum had been delivered to a safe port. A lot of work had still to be done to get the vessel fit for her passage through the Suez Canal to a European shipyard. The protruding plates had to be cut off and landed on deck and other minimum repairs made, but that is another story.

The salvage of the *Mare Nostrum* can only be described as an epic in the annals of post-war commercial salvage. The use of compressed air for lifting the ship when she was aground and for keeping her afloat is not new, but was carried out efficiently with the full appreciation that loss of pressure in the port tanks could result in a severe list and ultimately cause the vessel to capsize.

Perhaps the most remarkable feature was the tenacity and discipline of the small group of Dutchmen who succeeded not only in refloating a ship which others thought was a total loss, but did so with a minimum of manpower and equipment. It is not too difficult to understand that once this had been achieved, getting the main engine going and cleaning up the ship was a challenge that had to be accepted for the pure joy of doing a job well.

11   The salvage of the *Bretagne*

The Norwegian freighter *Bretagne*, 1340 G.R.T., was on her maiden voyage from Oslo to Rotterdam with general cargo. Her master and crew had not had much time to get to know her. On the morning of the 28th of March 1966, as the vessel approached the Dutch coast, she began to list severely to port. The weather at the time was extremely severe, with gale force winds and heavy seas.

At 0545 the same morning the master sent out a distress message as the list was increasing rapidly. Within minutes of receiving the message, the Wijsmuller tug *Titan* left Ijmuiden Harbour and nosed out into the gale. The weather conditions were appalling; so much so that the Ijmuiden pilot boat had suspended operations.

The Ijmuiden lifeboat *Neeltje Jacoba* was launched and also made her way towards the distressed cargo ship. Contact by radio was made with the *Titan*, and at 0645 the tug's offer of assistance was accepted by the captain of the *Bretagne* on the basis of Lloyd's Open Form. The tug was informed that at the time the distress message had been sent out, the little ship was 14 miles west of Ijmuiden, and heading for Ijmuiden at half speed with a 20 degree list to port. She was making water and in danger of capsizing. The *Titan* proceeded at full speed and came up to the ship just after 0615. In spite of weather conditions a line was passed to the stricken ship.

At 0645, the line was secured and the tug set course for Ijmuiden Piers with the *Bretagne* in tow, but in danger of capsizing at any minute, as her list to port increased. The master of the tug radioed a request to Ijmuiden Harbour Master for permission to enter the port, and duly received approval. At approximately 0830 the *Titan* got her tow inside the breakwater, and other Wijsmuller vessels including the *Nestor* came to assist in towing her towards the Averijhaven, where it was intended to beach the vessel to prevent capsizing.

By 0900 the vessel's list had increased to 40 degrees, and it was apparent to all concerned that she was heeling over more rapidly every minute as water entered her holds. By 1000 she was lying on her beam ends and the crew had climbed onto the upturned side at approximately the same time as the vessel was beached safely. They were then removed to safety.

The activity in the offices of the Bureau Wijsmuller was intense. It was appreciated that the *Bretagne* would have to be righted as quickly as possible, as mud and salt water would do irrevocable damage to her machinery and cargo. Divers were ordered to carry out a survey of the vessel and to close and seal off as many openings as possible to stop mud and water from entering. The owners and ship builders were contacted, and together with information provided by the master and crew, a detailed picture of the vessel and her cargo with its distribution, was built up. Part of the cargo which had got wet as a result of the water entering the holds commenced to give off noxious and inflammable gases, which had to be dealt with by providing ventilation and allowing it to escape. Meanwhile, the pumps and other equipment were being assembled to lift the vessel and pump her out.

The general plan was to use four 20-foot cantilever arms welded to the ship's side, to help lift the ship in conjunction with four 10-ton winches. It had been calculated that with the use of the cantilevers and the right set of six-sheave heavy duty blocks rove to advantage, the pull of the winches would each be increased to 100 tons. It was planned to use the winches in conjunction with the salvage vessel *Octopus* to lift the ship gradually, and at the same time to pump her out with a battery of pumps mounted on pontoons, and the tug *Nestor*. The winches had to be assembled and mounted on anchor points, which were constructed on the dunes by digging pits and providing the solid beds from which the winches could exert their full power without risk of slipping on the soft wet sand.

All of this could not be done. A host of equipment was needed. Several jobs went on simultaneously; mobile cranes fitted with grabs were hired to dig the anchor pits. Work went on day and night once the pits had been dug. Heavy timbers were placed in the pit and secured to make a firm base for each winch. Simultaneously the cantilevers were being constructed, and when finished were taken out to the ship, where they were carefully welded in position on the starboard side.

A great deal of water had entered the vessel's holds and engine room. To handle the water and assist with weight reduction while lifting her into an upright position, a hole was cut in the starboard quarter shell plating through which hoses could be led into the engine room. The pumps on the *Nestor* and various barges were thus able to pump the water out at rates approaching 2500 tons per hour.

Finally on the night of the 8th of April, the tackles were rigged, and the *Octopus* took up her position across the harbour, her heavy wires connected to the strong points on the submerged port side of the *Bretagne*. At 0430 Captain Ijsseling took up a position on the superstructure of the ship from which vantage point he could see both the *Octopus* and the winches. With the help of a portable radio he was in a good position to monitor the operation and measure progress as the vessel was slowly righted.

At 0500 on the 9th of April, which happened to be Easter Sunday, the lifting operation started. The winches on shore took the strain, and the *Octopus* tightened up her heavy lifting wires. Slowly the strain was increased while the pumps kept up a steady suction on the water in the ship. It was some time before any change was noticeable in the ship's position, but Captain Ijsseling was able to measure the progress and, to the relief of everybody involved, suddenly reported that the ship had moved and come up 3 degrees. Gradually she continued to move towards an upright position and having once broken suction, and getting the submerged port side off the muddy harbour bottom, steady progress was made.

The critical point was determined to be past when the vessel had come up to 20 degrees from the horizontal, but no major problems were experienced. Slowly, the combined efforts of the winches and the *Octopus*, righted the *Bretagne*, till at 1030 on the 9th, the ship had been pulled into a position which brought her hatches out of the water, and left her with a list of only 20 degrees to port. At this point the righting operation was stopped and the slack water removed from the engine room and other accessible locations. With the winches and the *Octopus* holding the vessel in this position, the hatch covers were carefully removed and three floating cranes commenced discharging the cargo into lighters. Loaded with general cargo, much of which had been damaged or destroyed by salt water, the operation was a delicate one and took nearly three weeks to complete as the cargo had to be sorted and removed with care and due regard to the stability of the ship, which was still aground on a tidal harbour bottom.

Gradually, as the cargo was discharged, more and more of the mud coated port side was uncovered. When finally the cargo discharge was completed and the *Bretagne* was refloated, she was left with only a slight list to port. After all the salvage equipment was removed, she was towed to Amsterdam for repairs with the cantilevers still welded to her starboard side.

In review, it has to be remembered that if prompt action had not been taken, the ship might have sunk outside the harbour and the operation of salving her would have been more difficult. Getting the vessel into shallow water inside the protection of the harbour was, therefore, a major factor in reducing the size and scope of the salvage operation. The risks of the ship sinking and obstructing the harbour entrance as she was towed in, cannot be overlooked. The final lifting of the ship was undertaken with the minimum loss of time, and the method used was traditional, combining pumps, shore winches and a heavy lift vessel.

12 The grounding and salvage of the *President Garcia*

The *President Garcia* flying the flag of the Philippines went aground in Saints Bay, Isle of Guernsey, in the Channel Islands, just before midnight on the 13th of July 1967. Loaded with 9500 tons of copra, her draft before grounding was reported to be 25 feet 6 inches forward and 29 feet 6 inches aft. She was proceeding up channel at full speed when the grounding took place.

News of the grounding was received in the Wijsmuller offices in Ijmuiden at 0130 on the 14th of July. Shortly afterwards orders were passed to the tug *Willem Barendsz*, which was stationed near Land's End, to proceed towards Guernsey. Steps were taken to contact the owner's Rotterdam agents, with a view to arranging for a salvage agreement to be signed, and a message was sent to the master of the *President Garcia* via the British shore station 'Niton Radio', offering the assistance of the tug *Willem Barendsz* 5,375 I.H.P. on the basis of Lloyd's Open Form. Another telex was sent to the owners in Manila informing them that Lloyds of London had reported that the ship had gone aground, and offering the assistance of the *Willem Barendsz*.

While the tug was proceeding to the help of the *President Garcia*, she relayed messages for the vessel's master and the owner's Rotterdam agent, which culminated in the latter agreeing to Lloyd's Open Form, subject to the owners in Manila approving the decision. Although the ship's master had reported to the Rotterdam agent that he was aground on sand, he also admitted in the same message that the forepeak and No. 3 starboard double bottom tank were leaking. This message, therefore, indicated that the vessel had either passed over something hard prior to grounding, or had run aground on something more than sand. After considering the situation, the decision was taken to send the *Utrecht*, which was anchored in Mounts Bay, to the scene of the grounding, as it began to look like a full scale salvage job. The *Willem Barendsz* arrived off St. Peter Port, and was actually in sight of the casualty by 1050 on the 14th of July, and after some delay obtained a pilot at about

1120. She then proceeded into Saints Bay where she anchored in about 7 fathoms of water.

Captain Kleingeld, master of the *Willem Barendsz*, then proceeded on board the stricken vessel by boat. He introduced himself to the master of the *President Garcia*, Captain Frederico Gutierrez, who gave him an up-to-date report on the situation. A check on the tanks and holds indicated that the forepeak was badly damaged, and No. 3 starboard double bottom containing fuel oil was leaking badly. No. 4 starboard double bottom was also leaking. This tank contained boiler water and the extent of the damage was hard to estimate. Soundings of Nos. 3 and 4 holds indicated that oil might be getting into these holds from minor leaks. The vessel was heading 285° True and she had a list of 3 degrees to port. The engine room was reported undamaged. The cargo consisted of copra in bulk:

No. 1 hold	...	1680 L tons
No. 2 hold	...	1850 L tons (including the four deep tanks)
No. 3 hold	...	2544 L tons
No. 4 hold	...	1933 L tons
No. 5 hold	...	1502 L tons

Soundings were taken all round the vessel and it became clear that she was aground at least partially on rock projecting under the ship from the starboard side abeam of No. 3 hold.

The master signed Lloyd's Open Form, and Captain Kleingeld returned to his tug. A report was sent to Ijmuiden on the condition of the *President Garcia*.

At 1530 on the 14th of July, the tug *Utrecht* arrived in the bay, and Kleingeld went on board to discuss the situation with her master, Captain Bronsdijk. A course of action was agreed between the two masters whereby the *Utrecht*'s diver would make a survey of the ship's bottom at half tide. They also agreed on the need to sound round the vessel in more detail, and investigate how best the ship could be towed off without damage from rocks in the near vicinity. The diver's inspection revealed that there was a large hole in the forepeak, estimated at 15 feet by 15 feet in area, caused by direct contact with rocks which partly obscured the hole. The hull was embedded in sand from forward to about half way along No. 1 hold. From this point the bottom was clear of the sand to approximately amidships, where the hull was again in contact with the bottom, which was mainly of sand.

As the diver moved aft, he found that the hull was aground on sand in the vicinity of Nos. 4 and 5 holds, but the stern and propeller were clear of the bottom. The diver confirmed rock under No. 3 hold and starboard bilge keel, but was unable to indicate how far it projected under the ship. The survey of the surrounding area indicated that there was very little room for the tugs to manoeuvre and pull the vessel off. At short distances off both quarters, rock clusters made the job a high risk. The ship had been lucky in going aground near to high water, and in not striking rock clusters heavily on the way in.

At 1700 hours the *Utrecht*'s 6-inch steel towing wire was connected to the *President Garcia* by means of a steel wire pennant which had been taken on board the vessel earlier. This action was taken as a precaution, and the tug anchored again as soon as the towing wire was connected. Both masters were in agreement that it was unlikely that the tugs could tow the ship off without first taking cargo out of No. 1 to lighten the ship. It was estimated that at least 1000 tons would have to be moved, unless the ship could trim more by the stern. They were also very concerned that the vessel would sustain damage with the big tidal rise and the unsupported section between No. 1 hold and the midships.

The problem was – could they afford to wait for the cargo to be moved, and risk the vessel cracking in the unsupported section? Finally, it was agreed that an attempt to tow off was justified and at 2320 the *Willem Barendsz* connected her towing gear to the stern of the *President Garcia* and commenced towing with the *Utrecht*, until both tugs were at full power. The wind was force 2 to 3, but a long 5-foot swell came into the bay during the high water period. Between half tide and low water, rocks and the shallow water tended to damp out the swell. At 0025 on the 15th, the ship reported that she had altered her heading 6° and was now 291° True. At 0115 the tugs stopped pulling and went to anchor, the attempt having failed.

At approximately 0600 on the 15th, a message was passed to Captain Kleingeld from the *President Garcia* to the effect that the vessel was beginning to crack forward. Kleingeld left his tug and proceeded to board. He found that his worst fears had been justified. As the tide fell, the ship had begun to sag in the unsupported area between No. 1 hold and amidships. As the time of low water approached, the stress had reached maximum values, and the hull and deck plating had started to give. He observed that deck plating had sagged across the full width of the vessel between the forward end of No. 2 hatch coaming and the deck housing. There was a crack in the deck plating between the two cargo winches, and these had partly sunk into the fold formed by the distorted plating. No. 2 hatch coaming had the forward end set in and was badly distorted.

Looking at the sheer strake on either side he found that there was a vertical fracture approximately 2 feet deep below which the steel plates were distorted as far as the waterline. Captain Kleingeld's inspection also revealed that the deck plating had been torn from the hull in the vicinity of the fracture on both sides. A diver was sent down but was unable to find further damage. It was apparent that the attempt to refloat the ship had moved the vessel about 18 feet to port, but the rock ledge in way of No. 3 still extended some distance under the ship, and the vessel was now listing 3 degrees to starboard.

The master of the *President Garcia* was inclined to blame the 'towing off attempt' for the split, and it took all Captain Kleingeld's patience and diplomacy to convince him that this was not the case, and that his ship had sagged and split because the section under No. 2 was unsupported. As the tide fell, maximum stress had occurred at low water not during high water when tugs had tried to pull her off.

Discussing the new developments with Ijmuiden on the radio telephone, agreement was reached that the vessel would have to be lightened, and Wijsmuller's office staff started to make arrangements for lighters or small coasters to be chartered to lighten the ship. With both No. 2 winches out of commission, it was also considered expedient to hire or buy a portable grain elevator to transfer cargo quickly. It was agreed that the best course of action for the two tugs was not to try to pull the vessel off at high water, but to steady her if she became lively, to stop her working and increasing the fracture. Captain Kleingeld was informed that Mr. Bylsma from Wijsmuller's head office would be arriving in Guernsey shortly, and that a Captain Gibson, London Salvage Association surveyor, was also expected on the scene the same day. Both men arrived around 1400 hours and a meeting was arranged on board the *President Garcia*.

The situation was reviewed step by step. A comparison of the soundings taken prior to grounding and those taken at 1200 on the 15th confirmed that the forepeak, No. 3 and No. 4 starboard double bottom tanks, were tidal. Soundings also indicated that water was entering the well in No. 3 hold. It was next agreed that approximately 100 tons of fuel oil would be transferred from No. 2 port

**PRESIDENT GARCIA
AGROUND IN SAINTS BAY**

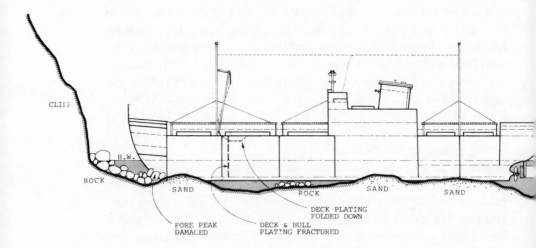

CLIFF

H.W.

ROCK

SAND   ROCK   SAND   SAND

DECK PLATING
FOLDED DOWN

FORE PEAK   DECK & HULL
DAMAGED   PLATING FRACTURED

and 4 starboard double bottom tanks to No. 4 deep tanks. This was done to reduce the amount of weight in the critical area, and to avoid unnecessary pollution if No. 2 port and starboard double bottoms became tidal. Soundings were taken around the vessel with a view to checking if shallow draft lighters and coasters could be brought alongside. As a result of these soundings it was agreed that a coaster with a maximum draft of 10 feet could get alongside Nos. 1 and 2 holds on the starboard side.

There was concern that No. 1 starboard deep tank was leaking and that the covers were not secured, as cargo had been loaded in both No. 1 port and starboard deep tanks. It was also found that the ship's pumps were not working effectively, and portable pumps were transferred from the *Utrecht* and *Willem Barendsz* to help handle water in the damaged compartments. A small amount of oil was found drifting around the *President Garcia*, and this was treated with solvent.

Late on the 15th of July, a message was received that a small coaster called the *Teunika* was on her way to take off part of the cargo. In addition, the tug *Stentor* was in the process of loading a portable grain elevator at Zeebrugge. This elevator was named 'Vac-u-Vator', and a special service mechanic would be sent to look after it. The *Stentor* was also bringing extra pumps and fire equipment in case the copra caught fire after becoming wet. On the 16th of July, further discussions resulted in agreement of all concerned to fill the afterpeak with ballast water, and to try to transfer more fuel from No. 2 double bottom tanks to No. 4 deep tanks. It was felt that these measures would help to reduce the buoyancy aft and stop the vessel working the fracture on the rising tide.

The situation in Nos. 1 and 2 holds and No. 1 starboard deep tank was a matter for much uneasy speculation. A suggestion was voiced that the duct keel could be used to inspect the forward compartments which could not be sounded. It would necessitate removing the manhole cover, which in itself was a risk, as the duct might be flooded, but if it was dry, a man could crawl forward along the duct and holes could be drilled to check if water had entered the compartments concerned. After some discussion, the chief engineer of the *Utrecht* volunteered to do the job.

The manhole cover was removed very cautiously, first by slacking one or two bolts, and then gradually easing the cover back. Some water was found in the duct, but this was apparently an accumulation over a period, for it was pumped out and the duct keel was found to be watertight. The chief engineer then crawled forward, equipped with a safety line, drill and wooden plugs. The first compartment to be checked was No. 1 port deep tank. This was found to be dry, and the hole was sealed with a wooden plug. Later No. 1 port double bottom tank and No. 1 hold were checked and found dry. Meanwhile, a careful check of No. 1 starboard deep tank, which could be sounded, revealed that the water level in the tank was slowly increasing.

It was fully appreciated that with the swell entering the bay, the ship could damage her bottom when she became lively on the rising tide. Steps were taken to cut off and plug all vent and sounding pipes into Nos. 1 and 2 port and starboard double bottoms. At a later stage Nos. 3 and 4 port and starboard double bottoms were dealt with in the same way. The idea was to obtain some flotation from trapped air if the tanks were holed, and to facilitate passing compressed air into the tanks if it became necessary. The local Wijsmuller agent was also requested to provide a number of used car tyres which could be hung over the side of the *President Garcia* to act as fenders between the ship and the coasters which were being chartered to offload some of the copra.

At about 2000 hours on the evening of the 16th, a new fracture was found on the starboard side in way of No. 1 deep tank, which was already known to be leaking. The fracture was about 4 feet above the low water level and proved impossible to plug, although attempts were made on successive days to fit wooden plugs at low water to stop water from entering as the tide began to rise. On the morning of the 17th, work was started, hanging fenders over the side, topping derricks at No. 3 hatch to get the 'Vac-u-Vator' on board. In addition, soundings were taken and the duct kept opened up and inspected. A new fold was discovered on the deck about 20 feet aft of the existing one, and the hull plating on the starboard side was also showing signs of a new fold or fracture. The diver was sent down, but was unable to report anything new. During the afternoon, oil was seen alongside in small quantities, and was sprayed with solvent. No. 2 hatch was opened up ready for discharge, and immediately the ship and surroundings became infested by a swarm of copra flies.

On the 18th at 0100 the *Stentor* arrived and Captain Kleingeld boarded and piloted her alongside. By 0500, the 'Vac-u-Vator' had been transferred, together with several other items such as fire and salvage pumps. A working party consisting of men from all three tug crews then commenced rigging the 'Vac-u-Vator'. It was moved, using tackles, until it was on the starboard side, and half way along No. 2 hatch. The suction and delivery piping was then connected, and the equipment tested and found to be working. The fire and salvage pumps were rigged in way of No. 4 hatch and both were tested and ran satisfactorily. Provision was also made to segregate wet copra aft in way of No. 5 hatch, where a rough wooden frame, consisting of wooden bulkheads had been made.

At 0930 the coaster *Teunika* arrived, and Captain Kleingeld piloted her alongside the *President Garcia*'s starboard side. At 1115 the discharge of cargo commenced with six men from the tugs' crews down in the hold shifting copra to the suction of the 'Vac-u-Vator'. By 1700 the first parcel of cargo, marked 'Davac', was discharged from the top of No. 2 hatch, and bundles of reeds were transferred to the coaster to provide the separation between the first and second parcel. Work continued right through the night, the work party from the tugs receiving no assistance from the crew of the *President Garcia*. By 1915 on the 19th of July, approximately 160 tons of copra had been transferred, and the *Teunika* had to leave as her draft was restricted by the limited amount of water alongside.

At 1930 the second coaster, the *Irene*, was brought alongside by Captain Kleingeld, and the transfer of copra continued. During the previous high water, the ship had become extremely lively, and

she had altered her heading to 295° True. It was hoped that enough
cargo from No. 2 would be transferred by 1600 hours on the 20th
of July to reach the tank top and seal the leaking starboard deep
tank; also to permit an attempt to refloat the ship at high water,
which occurred at 1845 hours on the 20th. Digging a hole in the
copra in No. 2 to reach the deep tank, slowed the discharge of cargo,
and also caused a certain amount of personal risk to the men in
the hold, as a movement of the ship could cause the copra to shift
and bury them.

A check at high water on the ship's draft marks indicated that
the waterline cut the mark at 19 feet 3 inches and 32 feet 00 inches.
Allowing for the least buoyancy, it was calculated that approximately 178 tons would have to be discharged. Work continued during the night, and at the same time plans were made to refloat the
ship.

The Harbour Master of St. Peter Port was requested to remove
all small yachts and boats from the vicinity. Two pumps were
rigged in series in No. 2 hold to deal with any water which might
enter the hold from the leaking deep tank. Rocks which might
endanger or hamper the tugs or the ship were buoyed, and in one
case marked by mooring one of the *Utrecht*'s boats over it, and
the master and chief engineer were requested to have the turbines
warmed through and a full head of steam available at least two
hours before the p.m. high water on the 20th.

The morning of the 20th of July dawned with fine weather and
a gentle southerly breeze, together with a light south west swell.
An inspection of No. 1 hold and the various double bottom tanks
was made via the duct keel, and the manhole was secured for the
last time. Soundings showed 19 feet of water in No. 2 starboard
deep tank. At 0905 the coaster *Canada* arrived and was told to
anchor. At about midday the list increased on the falling tide to
5 degrees and at 1400 hours *Irene* had to be shifted astern as she
was starting to touch a rock on the seabed.

During the afternoon two divers from the tugs *Utrecht* and *Stentor* were sent down for a final inspection. They indicated that the
rock abeam of No. 3 hold starboard side, was no longer in contact
with the bilge keel, but had left a large dent.

At 1500 the split in the hull by the deep tank was sealed with
a large joint of bacon, pulled home with fish bolts.

At 1530 the transfer of copra was stopped, and the *Irene* unmoored and went to anchor with about 100 tons of copra on board.
It should also be mentioned that No. 1 starboard deep tank coaming

was uncovered, but found to be badly buckled. A hole was dug into the copra in the deep tank and the suction pipes inserted from the two pumps in series, which were rigged to handle any serious leakage. The wet copra was placed on deck on the port side of No. 3 hatch as there was insufficient time to move it aft. The *Stentor* made fast alongside *President Garcia*'s starboard side at 1630. The second mate of the *Willem Barendsz*, equipped with a portable radio, and several other members of the salvage crew, remained on board.

At 1700 hours the *Willem Barendsz* and the *Utrecht* weighed anchor, and took the strain on their towing lines. By 1722 hours, both tugs were towing at full power. At 1730 the ship moved, her heading changing to 300° True. Four minutes later she was on 305° True, and slowly the starboard list reduced. At 1758 she was heading 318° True and was reported to be moving astern. The *President Garcia* was now getting fairly close to rocks on her port side, and it was necessary for the tugs to move round to the north as far as the limited room would permit. At 1809 she went slow astern on her engines and, shortly after, her head moved to 328° True.

At 1817 hours the ship suddenly came off and moved astern rapidly. The tugs stopped towing and put the engines full ahead, with rudder hard to starboard to check her, and to swing the stern to port. The engines were stopped as soon as the stern way was off, and the vessel lay motionless, heading north, while the *Stentor* unmoored and then moved round and made fast forward. By 1845 she was fast, and the *Utrecht* cast off at 1900 hours to provide the *Willem Barendsz* with more manoeuvring room. A report from the ship indicated that No. 1 starboard deep tank had started to fill as soon as the vessel was afloat, and was now overflowing into No. 2 starboard deep tank. The ship's bilge pump was operating on No. 2 deep tank, and the two pumps rigged in series were also started. While the pumps kept the inflowing sea water under control, the margin of safety was not high and more portable pumps and men were transferred to the ship from *Utrecht* and *Willem Barendsz*.

As these pumps were being transferred, the tugs nursed the ship into St. Peter Port roadstead where she anchored at 2030 hours. The tugs cast off and the divers were sent down at 2130 to do a bottom inspection. They discovered a new fold near the existing one, and a fracture on the starboard side. The latter was sealed by 2230 using wooden wedges. The current and tide was running at 5 knots, hampering the divers, and one broke loose and had to be rescued with a launch. The *Irene* sailed for Rotterdam, but *Canada* was kept standing by at anchor. The additional pumps were connected up and with their aid, the situation was well under control. To stop the pump suctions from blocking, a perforated drum was used to protect the suction pipes. A continuous watch was kept on No. 2 hold, but most of the time the water level was maintained 6 feet below the deep tank coaming. The motor lifeboat, which had been used to mark the rock in Saints Bay, was used to collect the buoys and other equipment used in getting the vessel afloat.

At a meeting on board the *President Garcia*, it was agreed that St. Peter Port was not a safe port for this size of vessel, and that the ship should be towed stern first to Rotterdam, which was her original destination, and where she could be repaired after the cargo was discharged. As a precaution, and to make sure that the leaking deep tank in No. 2 was accessible at all times, the hole dug in the copra was shored up with timber.

On the 21st, a working party from all three tugs commenced work plugging fractures with wooden plugs. Fuel, food and supplies were transferred from the tugs to the ship for the use of the salvage team. In addition, the afterpeak was pumped out to reduce the stern trim. After a final divers' inspection the tow commenced at 1800 hours, with the *Willem Barendsz* and the *Utrecht* connected to the stern, and the *Stentor* forward acting as a rudder, while the vessel moved out to sea slowly, sheering from side to side. The *Canada* had been dismissed earlier as there was no need for her services.

The tow, as expected in the circumstances, made slow progress, but the weather remained good and the ship reached Rotterdam on the 24th of July, entering the port at 1341, and arriving off the Rotterdam Drydock Company's shipyard at 1550. At this point the Wijsmuller tugs handed over to river tugs which towed the vessel into the Wusthaven where she was moored to the buoys. At 1830 the certificate of delivery was signed, which ended a successful salvage job that had been conducted with great skill.

It can now be said that the first effort to tow the ship off was probably premature, but might have been successful. It might also have led to the ship striking other rocks in deeper water with disastrous consequences. The main effort was well planned and executed, and the use of the 'Vac-u-Vator' was ingenious.

13 The *Torrey Canyon*

Not all salvage attempts are successful. A case in point was the *Torrey Canyon*, which ran aground on the 18th of March 1967. The vessel was a 118,000 D.W.T. tanker, loaded with crude oil and bound for Swansea from the Middle East.

She grounded on the Seven Stones, one of the many outlying groups of rocky shoals that guard the approaches to the Scilly Isles off the south western extremities of the British Isles. In March the weather can be very severe, with gale force winds and heavy seas, coupled with high swells that roll in from the Atlantic. The ship ran aground at, or near, full speed, and as a result did considerable damage to her bottom. This in turn led to oil leaking into the sea in vast quantities, so that the neighbouring fishing grounds and beaches were threatened by extensive pollution. The stranding was a major disaster, and there is no doubt that the oil spilt caused a great deal of damage, but had the vessel been salvaged safely, the amount of oil that was spilt would have been greatly reduced, and this alone justified the attempt to salve her.

Shortly after grounding, the *Torrey Canyon* sent out a distress message asking for immediate assistance. The Wijsmuller tug *Utrecht*, stationed in Mounts Bay, acknowledged the call and immediately set out to the assistance of the stranded vessel. The ship's master was unwilling to agree to assistance rendered on the basis of Lloyd's Open Form, and there was some delay before Wijsmuller's office in Ijmuiden was able to contact the owners and get agreement. Once this was obtained, the tugs *Stentor* and *Titan* were diverted to assist the *Utrecht*, while a salvage crew of experts were mobilised in Ijmuiden ready to fly to the scene of the disaster, together with a great deal of equipment.

Three planes were chartered, and men and equipment were flown to Exeter, and then transported to Mounts Bay to join the waiting tugs. Some equipment was taken on to the small airfield at Land's End ready to be flown direct to the striken ship. The salvage team was led by Captain H. B. Stal, who lost his life whilst supervising the salvage operation.

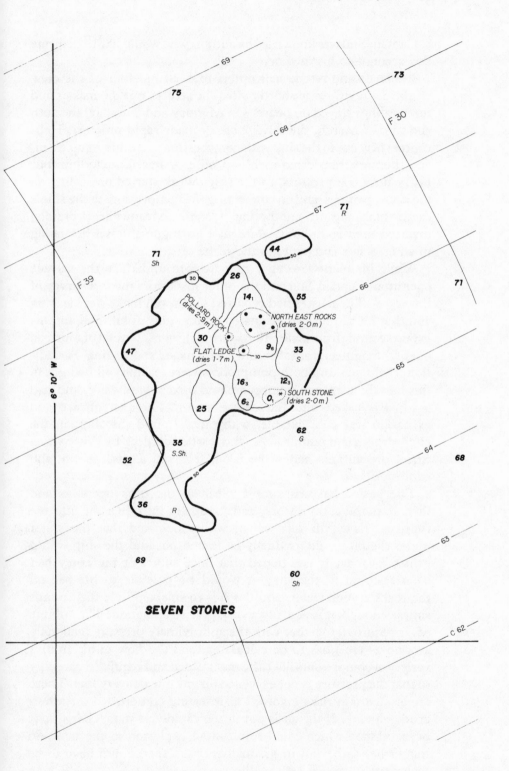

Captain Stal was known to the author, who would like to dedicate this account to his memory.

Lifeboats and rescue helicopters took all but four of the crew off the *Torrey Canyon* shortly after she struck, but the master and three ratings stayed on board. On Monday and Tuesday, the 20th and 21st of March, the salvage crews made rapid progress. Helicopters flew out to the ship with compressors and other equipment, and the tugs transferred men and other material, including four heavy duty compressors, to the ship. Work started on sealing all the deck openings, and on connecting the compressors to the ship's cargo tank steam smothering system. Meanwhile Ijmuiden diverted the tug *Praia da Adraga*, a Portuguese vessel belonging to an associate company, to the scene of the disaster.

While his men were busy preparing to undertake the salvage operation, Captain Stal and the other inspectors made a survey of the vessel. The master had reported that seven tanks were leaking and that he had lost an estimated 30,000 tons of oil. Stal and his experts found that the situation was much worse. A total of fourteen out of the eighteen cargo tanks were damaged and leaking. In addition, fuel tanks and both pumprooms were leaking; oil had got in through the damaged pumproom and mixed with water, and had gradually leaked into the engine room. The risk of fire and explosion was considerable, with oil all round the ship, in the engine room and pumprooms, and washed on deck by every wave. Strict precautions had to be taken to avoid all risk of fire and explosion.

The basic plan was simple. Seal all the deck openings and then start the compressors, and gradually introduce air into the ruptured tanks. In this way it was anticipated that the water under the oil would gradually be forced out and the ship would gain buoyancy. It was hoped that once sufficient buoyancy had been restored to the ship, it would be possible to lift her off the rocks at high water, and tow her to safety. While this sounds simple enough, it is actually a very precise operation. The volume of air required, together with the approximate pressure (generally around 2–3 lb.) has to be calculated, and the flow of air from a variety of compressors has to be manifolded and regulated carefully so that the pressure is not exceeded on any one delivery line. There are also certain risks involved in inserting compressed air into a crude oil tank. If the air is put in too rapidly, a static charge may be developed which could result in an explosion in the tank. So the air has to be put in gradually. Leaks appear and have to be sealed off.

The men work under a great deal of tension, even though they may be used to running risks. Nobody wants to die on a stranded oil tanker which, if it catches fire, could mean everyone being burnt to death on board, or in the oil-covered water around the ship. The *Torrey Canyon* attracted a lot of publicity in the world press, but little was said about the professional salvage teams and the work they were doing. In fact, many papers gave the impression that the British Government were directing the salvage operation with the Royal Navy actually doing the work. This of course was not true. The Government and the Royal Navy were kept informed, and agreed all the measures taken, but the actual work was left to the professional salvage crews.

Captain Stal hoped to make the first attempt to get the vessel off on Tuesday, or at the latest Wednesday the 22nd. Tragically on Wednesday, there was a heavy explosion in the deserted engine room which caused Captain Stal and one of the crew of the *Praia da Adraga* to be blown overboard into the oily sea. Thanks to the bravery of sailors F. M. van Rixel and C. van Wijk, who dived in after them, both men were rescued, but Captain Stal later died on board the *Titan* in spite of the doctor flown out by helicopter to attend him.

The explosion prompted the withdrawal of the salvage crew from the wreck for the time being. Ijmuiden placed Mr. H. Bijsma in charge of the operation while Mr. P. van de Berg coordinated the operation with the authorities ashore. Work was resumed on Wednesday the 22nd of March with the object of lifting the vessel off on Thursday the 23rd, but weather conditions hindered work, and it was not until Saturday the 25th that an attempt was made. All four tugs were connected up and began to try working the ship off the rocks as the tide rose. While she appeared to float and move, the rocks on which she was impaled held her fast. Work was only undertaken during the hours of daylight, and the crews were taken off at night. On Sunday another attempt was made, again without success, and had to be stopped due to the rapidly deteriorating weather.

On the 26th, Easter Sunday, the ship began to break up and by evening the stern half had settled in the water so that the funnel was awash. On Easter Monday the forward section broke in two as a result of the huge seas which pounded over and against the hull. The wreck was inspected from the air by senior personnel from Bureau Wijsmuller with a view to the possible salvage of any or all of the three parts, but any attempt to do more was prevented by the Royal Navy, who ordered the tugs to leave the vicinity, while the R.A.F. attempted to set the wreck on fire by bombing. This proved exceedingly difficult to do, as the crude oil had weathered, and the cold sea temperature of the waves washing over the wreck supplied ideal coolant.

Apart from the failure of the salvage operation, and the loss of Captain Stal, Wijsmuller lost a lot of equipment on the *Torrey Canyon* and on the basis of Lloyd's Open Form – 'No Cure, No Pay' – had no means of recovering the cost of the equipment or the expense of such items as helicopter and aircraft charter hire.

14 Fire and salvage in the North Atlantic – *Etnefjell*

Among professional seamen the trade routes that cross the northern reaches of the Atlantic and Pacific have become notorious as places to avoid in winter. As the sun goes south of the Equator the days grow shorter and the weather deteriorates, making these lonely wastes of water inhospitable and forbidding. A merchant vessel which is unfortunate enough to experience trouble in such areas is a long way from help, and frequently ships have been known to go down with all hands before assistance arrives.

The *Etnefjell*, a Norwegian cargo ship, experienced an explosion in the engine room in Latitude 55° 20′ North and Longitude 30° 25′ West. The resulting fire burnt fiercely in the gale force winds, and the master sent out a distress message. This was picked up at Ijmuiden by Bureau Wijsmuller and relayed to the *Groningen* which was cruising on a mobile salvage station designated by the company, at slow speed. The tug was between the 46th and 47th parallels North, and cruising at slow speed between Longitudes 20° and 30° West. She started her second engine and set course for the position given, in spite of the bad weather. A south westerly gale was blowing with a high sea running. At noon on the 3rd of November 1968 she was in 46° 17½′ North, 29° 36′ West and trying hard to contact the burning vessel, but all her efforts were in vain.

On the 4th, the weather worsened till a full gale was blowing making the tug roll and heave as she plunged into the giant Atlantic waves. No contact with the ship was made that day, and those on board the tug began to wonder if she had sunk or been abandoned. The bad weather continued on the 5th of November, but the tug was making steady progress, and the U.S. Coastguard cutter *Absecon* responded to her radio messages indicating that she was in contact with the burning ship, and was able to supply valuable radio bearings to direct her to the vicinity. As a result of the close work between the two ships, the *Groningen* picked up the *Etnefjell* on her radar at 0140 on the 6th, and shortly afterwards identified the Coastguard cutter. On reaching the *Etnefjell* the tug steamed around the smitten ship, noticing that the rudder lay hard to starboard, and that she appeared to be gutted completely aft.

Steaming down to leeward of the vessel, she prepared and swung out a motor launch so that help could be ferried over to the cargo ship. At 0255 the boat was launched under the second mate. The second engineer and three seamen accompanied him. The second mate and one of the seamen had orders to board the *Etnefjell* and make an inspection, after which they were to communicate with the tug. The two men were put on board without major incident, but at 0345 when the boat returned to the *Groningen*, its rudder and tiller were unshipped and lost as the boat was hoisted out of the sea. The second mate reported that the master, chief engineer and first mate were still on board, and that he considered that with their help it would be possible to connect up a suitable towing pennant. Preparations went ahead on both ships to connect the tow.

By 0515 everything was in readiness, and taking advantage of a slight drop in the wind, the tug nosed into the northerly swell, and angled towards the bow of the *Etnefjell*, getting as close as possible so that the connection could be made. With no power on the ship, it was a major job to rig the towing gear, which consisted of 150 feet of 4½-inch wire, the end of which was secured to a set of bitts on board; 150 feet of 14-inch nylon were connected to the towing pennant, and this in turn was shackled into the 6-inch towing wire. The *Groningen* kept position slightly to windward of the tow, with her stern only a few feet from the lunging bow of the *Etnefjell*.

Slowly the wire pennant was pulled up and made fast, and, with decks awash the tug commenced paying out the nylon pennant, then the towing wire; the towing wire was paid out and chafing cradles secured at points where the wire made contact with the towing bars and tug's rail. By 0600 everything was in readiness, and the tug set course for Newfoundland after getting a fix from the *Absecon*, this vessel being equipped with Loran. The *Absecon* signalled 'Farewell', and left the tug and her tow in the faint light of the winter morning. The position provided by the cutter was approximately 55° North and 39° West.

After working up to cruising speed, the master of the *Groningen* called up his second mate and suggested that a thorough inspection of the ship should be undertaken as soon as possible, and a report made back to the tug so that the head office in Ijmuiden could be informed. This inspection revealed that the forepeak was dry, together with hold Nos. 4 and 5 and the after cofferdam, but there was approximately 1 foot of water in Nos. 1, 2 and 3 holds and in the engine room. The after accommodation was completely gutted and portholes warped with broken or melted ports, which made it impossible to seal them off against the weather.

The body of a crew member was found in the engine room, burnt and charred beyond all recognition. It was recovered and wrapped in canvas prior to stowing in a safe place. After receiving the report, the captain of the *Groningen* radioed Ijmuiden and was ordered to alter course for Falmouth. It was also necessary to plan another visit to the ship, as the five men on board had very little food on which to survive.

On the 6th of November weather conditions were judged to be good enough, and at 0900 the motor boat was launched under command of the chief mate. The equipment included bed clothes, food and some gas bottles for heating. The *Groningen* also had radio communication with the *Absecon*, reporting the change of plan and giving her their position. The boat was recovered without incident.

On the 7th, by 0800 the tug estimated her position to be 54° 21′ North and 34° 59′ West. The barometer was dropping and the wind and sea gradually increasing. It was decided to send more supplies across to the tow in case the bad weather lasted for any length of time. This was accomplished without incident, and proved to be timely. By noon the wind had reached force 7 and was increasing. Both ships were pitching and the tow was falling off to starboard, which had been anticipated as the rudder was jammed 45 degrees to starboard. At 1730 the swell increased and speed had to be reduced. The tow reported that everything was well, as both vessels plowed into the easterly gale. The bad weather continued during the 8th, freshening to force 8/9 and slowly veering to the south east. Speed was again reduced as the towing gear was starting to give problems. The wire cradle on the aftermost towing rail was crushed and washed overboard by heavy seas, and it began to look as though the tow line might part.

The weather continued to deteriorate and the motion of both ships became more violent. At 0830, the closing plate in a freeing port carried away as a result of heavy seas breaking over the towing deck. At 1140 the pennant parted in the *Etnefjell*'s chock. The tug crew were left with the job of recovering the towing gear in wild weather, while the five men on board the ship were requested to find and rig some lengths of chain to which the towing pennant could be secured, so that the chain would take the wear in the chock. Eventually, two lengths of chain about 30 feet long were found and dragged on to the foc'sle by the five exhausted men on the *Etnefjell*. Slipping and sliding as the ship rolled and plunged, they secured the chains to the anchor cables in front of the windlass, and for additional safety shackled in wires which were in turn secured to the ship's bitts.

Around midday an attempt was made to pass a $5\frac{1}{2}$-inch steel pennant on board, but this failed as it proved too heavy for the men on board to handle. A $4\frac{1}{2}$-inch pennant was also tried, but again failed. The plain pennant without a hawser was passed up, and with the aid of a tackle, secured to the chain. The pennant was retained on board until the weather moderated, and another attempt could be made. Connection was finally made on the 9th of November, and the *Groningen* set out once more for Falmouth. The tow was rolling 10 degrees, and sheering up to 20 degrees to starboard. All went well until the 11th, when the tug and tow ran into another gale, this time from the north north east. Speed was reduced gradually as the weather worsened to a strong gale. From time to time the tug had contact by radio telephone with Bureau Wijsmuller, and as a result the *Utrecht* was despatched to assist with the tow and to provide bunkers for *Groningen*. Two runners were also despatched on the *Utrecht* as it was felt that the five men on the ship needed reinforcement.

The weather continued to be bad, and a number of cradles were damaged, and one lost overboard when a heavy sea crossed the towing deck at the same time as the towing wire came down on the towing rail. The tow sheered violently, and progress was slow. On the 12th the dead reckoned position passed to Ijmuiden was 52° 20′ North and 25° 30′ West. On the 13th the gale was still blowing but had switched to east by south and forced a further reduction in speed. Weather continued at the same level throughout that night, with both vessels rolling heavily, but otherwise behaving well. It was estimated that the sea height reached 25–30 feet during the 14th.

At 2000 hours on the night of the 14th the *Etnefjell* reported that the towing chain had slipped, and that the starboard anchor was sagging out of the hawsepipe. The weight was taken off the tow line to give those on board a chance to secure the towing chains and anchor chains with additional wires. On the 15th the weather at last started to moderate. Those on board the tow were able to connect a grommet around one of the flukes of the anchor which had come clear of the hawsepipe and, with the aid of a tackle, to heave it home and secure it.

Radio communication was also established with the *Utrecht*, which was bringing bunkers and runners to the *Groningen*. On the 16th in approximately 51° 28′ North and 17° 26′ West visual contact was made with the *Utrecht* which, at 1130, closed with the *Etnefjell* and managed to get one of the runners across. The wind was moderating but the sea was confused and there was still a heavy swell running. To get a runner across meant passing a safety line to the ship, and the runner, wearing a wet suit, jumping off the tug and swimming to the *Etnefjell* where he was hauled aboard. In the circumstances the *Utrecht* was unable to bunker the *Groningen*, and connected to the *Groningen*'s bow to assist with towing. In doing so, her stern touched one of *Groningen*'s anchors, but luckily no damage was done.

On the 17th the wind freshened again until it was blowing from the south east at gale force 9. Both tugs continued doggedly towing to the east. The rudder of the *Etnefjell* had somehow moved, and was now jammed over to port, causing the ship to stay continuously over to port from the line of tow. On the 18th the bunker situation on board the *Groningen* was becoming critical, and some discussion took place with Ijmuiden and the other tug regarding the alternatives of the *Utrecht* taking over the tow while the *Groningen* went to Cork for bunkers, or alternatively making another attempt to pass bunkers from one to the other.

Fortunately the weather continued to moderate, and around 1700 the *Utrecht* was ready to pass her hose aboard the other tug. By 2100 the *Groningen* was receiving bunkers, and by 0225 on the 19th had received a total of 60 tons. After completing bunkers, the *Utrecht* stood by and escorted *Groningen* towards the English Channel. The weather was squally with winds sometimes gusting to force 8.

On Wednesday the 20th of November, the weather moderated, and as daylight approached it was decided to lower a boat and send some stores over to the ship. The motor boat was launched successfully, and went across to the *Utrecht* to pick up the additional runner before proceeding alongside the *Etnefjell*. Stores were transferred and the boat returned without incident. The 21st saw both tugs and the tow in the approaches to the English Channel. The noon position by Decca was found to be 49° 38.5′ North and 6° 57.5′ West. The wind was still from the south east and squally.

Friday the 22nd dawned with the *Groningen* preparing to hand over her tow to the harbour tugs in the approaches to Falmouth. The towing wire was gradually hove in, and at approximately 0920, pilots boarded the tug and the ship. A launch came alongside the *Etnefjell* with some additional boatmen to assist in mooring her. Shortly afterwards the local tug boat *St. Mawes* put a line on board, and assisted the *Groningen* to tow the vessel into Falmouth.

The salvage of the *Etnefjell* is typical of the hard operating conditions experienced by salvage crews on tugs working in the North Atlantic. The *Groningen* was very unfortunate in meeting gale force winds from the east. This undoubtedly slowed the tow and caused the anxiety over bunkers.

With the heavy weather experienced and the lack of power on the tow, it is remarkable that the tow line only parted once and the connection was made so rapidly.

15   The stranding and salvage of the *Elwood Mead*

Salvage is a field of human endeavour where comparison is difficult, if not impossible. The epics in the world of salvage are jewels,
but there are no real scales by which one can be weighed against
another, except perhaps in terms of skills used and the value of
vessel or cargo saved. Material values and technical skills are not
in themselves the only things that go to make an epic salvage job.
The circumstances and environment play a big part, as well as the
courage and the tenacity of those involved in such larger than life
dramas.

The *Elwood Mead* was loaded with iron ore – approximately
125,000 tons. She was on her maiden voyage from Port Dampier
to discharge in Rotterdam and Dunkirk, and ran aground on the
25th of December, 1973, on the reef-strewn coast of Guernsey in
the Channel Islands. The stranding occurred during the hours of
darkness, just after midnight.

The salvage operation that was mounted, really had three separate phases. The first phase involved the examination of the stranded
vessel and its surroundings, to assess whether the vessel and its
cargo could be saved. It also included the signing of the salvage
agreement, and the transfer of men and equipment to the vessel.
The second phase can be divided into two parts. First, the unsuccessful early attempts to get the vessel off before the weather
deteriorated. Secondly, the flooding of the engine room, followed
by the long drawn out effort to lighten the vessel, which culminated
in her being successfully refloated and towed out to deep water.
The third and final phase was the tow to Rotterdam and the cargo
lightering operation that took place off that port before the vessel
was finally permitted to enter.

This particular operations is well documented. As far as the
author is aware, it is the only one that has been extensively recorded
on live film cameras with the authentic sound effect of a ship working on the rocks in bad weather, and actually showing the hazardous
nature of the work. That the weather was bad cannot be in doubt
as, apart from the live film and ship's log, the Cypriot ship

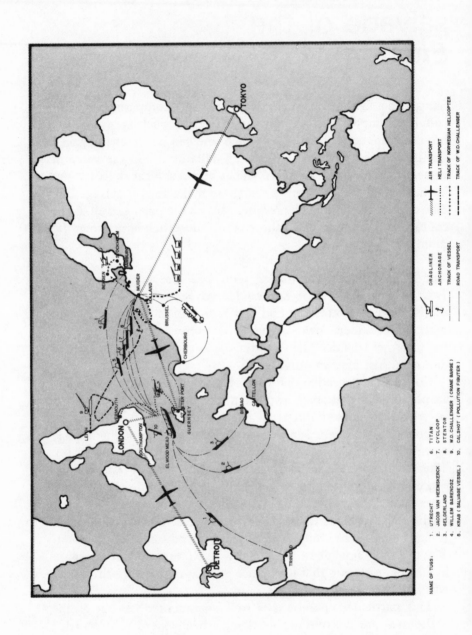

Prosperity foundered with all hands just a mile away from the grounded *Elwood Mead* during one of the many winter gales.

Mr. Nan Halfweeg, a senior salvage inspector employed by the Bureau Wijsmuller, was in charge of the operation. On the 28th of December, in company with the owner's representatives, he boarded the vessel and made a careful study of the situation. Using a local diving company he had the bottom inspected, while he himself made a careful inspection of the ship, her engine room, cargo holds, tanks and other spaces. The master and officers were also interviewed. As a result of this survey Mr. Halfweeg was left with no illusions – the ship was very badly damaged. The bottom had been pierced by rocks along most of her length and some rocks had actually penetrated up into the ship. In addition, examination of the chart indicated that she was surrounded by rocks, so that even if the efforts to refloat her were successful, difficulty might be experienced getting her back to deep water. On the brighter side, the engine room was still intact and therefore ship's power was available.

Back ashore he called Wijsmuller's head office and indicated that if the *Elwood Mead* was to be salvaged, it would take a major operation to do it. Manpower and equipment would be needed, and the necessary vessels to assist. Equipment would have to be flown into Guernsey and then conveyed out to the ship by small vessels in good weather and by helicopter if the weather was rough. Speed was essential as a winter gale could put the ship beyond help.

Halfweeg's plan was based on rapid mobilisation of craft and equipment. He planned to use pumps and compressors to lighten the ship of some 55,000 tons of salt water and then use a high tide to lift her off the rocks prior to towing out into deep water. Ijmuiden agreed to the plan, and work commenced as soon as the owners had agreed to sign the salvage agreement. A number of generators and compressors were hired locally, or bought and transferred to the *Elwood Mead* by small craft hired for the purpose. It was intended that the *Cycloop*, *Titan* and *Krab* would all assist in the operation. Work commenced on an attempt to drain leaking fuel tanks to stop oil pollution, but this was largely unsuccessful as the fuel was too cold and thick. At the same time tank tops were made watertight and generators and compressors connected up.

On the 31st of December the *Cycloop* arrived in Guernsey. More equipment was unloaded and shipped to the stranded vessel and the *Cycloop*'s motor boat commenced a survey of the area around the ship with an electronic echo sounder to try to locate a safe way

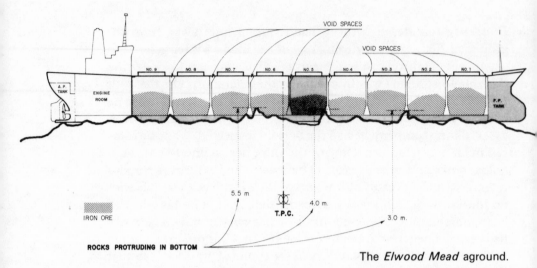

The *Elwood Mead* aground.

to tow the ship to deep water. Arrangements were made for meteorological data to be passed to Mr. Halfweeg, and a careful evaluation of tidal data was made. Although the tides were relatively small (neaps), it was decided to make an attempt to refloat as soon as all the double bottoms had been pressurised, as the weather was expected to deteriorate.

On the 1st of January good progress was made. Pumps were installed to empty No. 5 hold and a number of others were lowered into the void spaces between the holds. Air hoses were secured to the double bottoms and connected to the compressors, while the portable generators were started and tested.

At 1900 hours the tug *Titan* arrived and more hoses and pumps were transferred to the ship. On the 2nd of January the salvage vessel *Krab* arrived and came alongside with additional equipment, and by 1900 the pumps were started to pump out No. 5 hold and the flooded void spaces. At 2200 hours the compressors were started and it was calculated that it would take 15–20 hours to pressure the double bottoms to obtain flotation, and the timing was set to coincide with high water on the 3rd. It was anticipated that:

i)   26,000 tons of water would be pressurised out of the double bottoms.

ii)   29,000 tons would be pumped out of No. 5 hold, the void spaces and various other compartments.

On the 3rd at 0600, the *Calshot*, an oil pollution control boat, stood by with pollution equipment to handle any oil escaping from the ship, while the tugs *Willem Barendsz*, *Cycloop* and *Titan* connected their towing gear to the ship. The ship's rudder was secured by divers using 6-inch circumference wires. Between 0815 and 1345 hours several attempts were made to tow the vessel off, using all the tugs and the ship's engines, but though the ship became very lively and the heading changed, the pinnacles of rock on which she was impaled, held her firmly. As the tide began to fall the attempt was cancelled, though deballasting continued. At 2245 the tugs made another attempt, though weather conditions were getting steadily worse, but at 0120 on the 4th a report was received from the engine room that water was flooding into the engine room bilges through a hole in the duct keel. Divers tried to stem the leak with various plugs and by shoring up the leak with wooden beams, but to no avail.

At 0330 the refloating attempt was cancelled and the towing wires from the tugs disconnected. To hold the ship steady in the worsening weather conditions, the discharge of ballast was stopped and then the process was reversed as it became obvious that more ballast would be required to hold the ship steady. Divers inspected the engine room and found that a low level alarm on the duct keel had come off its mounting, thus allowing water to enter the engine room. At a meeting held on board it was decided to proceed with the salvage operation despite the setback, and to try to preserve and protect the machinery and electrical equipment in the engine room. A message was sent to Ijmuiden indicating that more equipment would be needed and that the engine room was flooded.

On the 5th of January the majority of the ship's crew were taken off and repatriated, leaving the master and a few deck and engineer officers. Divers were sent down to close all seacocks and valves in the engine room and to examine how best to patch the hole that had caused the trouble. The vessel was now labouring in a long western ocean swell estimated at about 15 feet, and was shipping a lot of water during the high tide periods. It was noted that the deck plating between Nos. 5 and 6 hatch covers had begun to buckle. The next day was spent in securing equipment against the weather and working in the engine room, whilst Wijsmuller's office in Ijmuiden organised a chartered flight with extra generators and other equipment.

On the 7th the bad weather continued, and hold Nos. 6 and 7 sprang leaks. The salvage crew were now mainly engaged in rescue operations which consisted of removing what salvage equipment they could from exposed locations to places of safety.

The 8th of January was a particularly bad day as wind, sea and swell worked round to the north west. Estimates indicate that the wind was force 8 gusting to 10, and the sea and swell 18 feet high. Portholes in the cabins on the boat deck were forced by the weather and had to be patched with steel plates.

The weather continued to cause great concern and hinder work until the 17th. The helicopter flew continuously between the shore and the ship with equipment, and on the 15th a new patch designed ashore was flown out and fitted by divers to the leak in the engine room; it was tested and held. Six submersible pumps were fitted and the work of reducing the water level in the engine room commenced. Specialists were flown in to Guernsey to work on the protection of the machinery as soon as conditions improved. A leak suspected in No. 4 hold on the 14th was confirmed on the 15th by soundings. On the 17th the weather started to moderate, but the *Prosperity*, referred to previously, foundered within sight of those on the *Elwood Mead*, with the loss of all hands. On board the *Elwood Mead* the rudder broke loose from its lashings.

With the vessel developing so many new leaks, it became evident that it would be necessary to discharge overboard some of the iron ore. The idea of using sand pumps was tested at a steel mill in Holland and worked successfully, and several of these pumps were shipped to Guernsey. They were flown out by the helicopter and the salvage team got ready to assemble them. On the 18th, the *Krab* returned from Cherbourg to St. Peter Port with more equipment. On board work started on assembling and hooking up portable generators in the engine room. By the 19th two 6-inch pumps were working and lowered the water to the level in the generating flat. The sand pump, assembled and installed in hold No. 7, was tested, and with improved hose was discharging iron ore in a slurry overboard. Work on the ship's generators started with the specialists working to remove or protect the equipment which had been covered by salt water.

On the 20th another sand pump was installed in No. 6 cargo hold and commenced discharging ore. In addition the lighting in the accommodation was hooked up to the portable generators. The *Krab* was able to get alongside and deliver two heavy generating units. The salvage crew were kept busy as the sand pumps and hoses kept giving trouble due to the abrasive nature of the ore. Work continued intermittently during lulls in the weather, but on the 28th all ore pumping operations had to be suspended due to the weather. The wind was force 10 and big seas were sweeping the decks doing considerable damage to the deck fittings and making the ship work. On the credit side, the ship's auxiliary diesel was started and worked successfully after cleaning and overhauling. During this period a lot of the ship's electrical equipment was removed ashore by helicopter and sent to Rotterdam for overhaul.

On the 29th of January with the weather moderating slightly, work was started on repairing the air vents and goose necks that had been damaged by the big seas. These were sealed and made watertight. In spite of the problems with the sand pumps, two pumps were kept in more or less continuous service. The cost of replacement was high, as three pumps were worn out, together with twenty one hoses and other equipment. Due to the discharge of ore and the reduction in the water level in the engine room, the vessel began to feel lively aft and it was decided to fill the engine room fuel tanks with water.

Work continued on the 30th and 31st, but hold Nos. 3 and 4 filled continuously with water due to the fact that the decks were awash at high tide and both decks and hatch covers leaked badly. On the 1st of February the *Krab* returned to the vessel from Cherbourg and managed to put more sand pumps and equipment on board and take off damaged equipment for repair. Before leaving she put diesel bunkers aboard the stranded vessel to keep the generators going. Shortly after she left, the weather deteriorated and caused pumping operations to be suspended. At 2230 hours the starboard bunker hatch cover was torn loose and dislocated by heavy seas. On the 2nd of February the low water periods were used to work on deck, securing and recovering salvage gear, making temporary repairs and reinforcing damaged hatch covers. On the 3rd, the *Krab* came alongside again in a lull in the weather and refuelled the stranded ship. An additional six pumps were put on board, together with two winches, while a lot more electrical equipment was offloaded so that it could be shipped to Rotterdam. Work was also started on welding heavy duty lugs on the deck to take the beach gear.

On the 4th of February the diesel-driven winches were welded to the decks and double bottom tanks 3, 4 and 5 were pressurised in turn to test the system. On the 5th, the *Krab* made an abortive attempt to run out the ground tackles; the sea was too rough and gradually conditions deteriorated. Vulnerable equipment was removed from the main deck and the rest lashed down as securely as conditions permitted. By the morning of the 6th it was blowing force 11 and the helicopter was unable to fly. Four of the windows

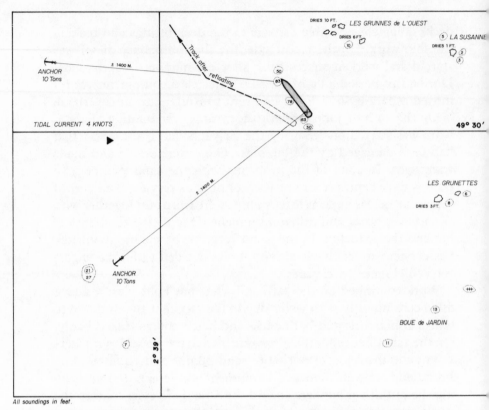

The layout of the ground tackle used in salvaging the *Elwood Mead*.

on the bridge deck were smashed and the accommodation flooded. The ship was working and straining badly all the time and a lot of the salvage gear was lost overboard.

By the morning of the 7th the wind and sea had eased sufficiently for those on board to take stock of the situation. The ship was in a much worse state than at any time before. There were signs of deck plate buckling and small fractures between all the hatch covers aft of No. 2, and much equipment had been lost or damaged. Work commenced on cleaning up the mess, repairing the salvage gear, making temporary repairs to deck fittings and plugging leaks.

On the 8th of February the *Krab* managed to lay the forward ground tackle which consisted of a 9½-ton anchor and 1200 feet of 6-inch wire. It now became a race against time. The next set of big tides was due on the 11th, but much had to be done and many hours were lost at or near high water, when the sea continued to break over the ship. Gradually, hope of getting her off on the 11th dwindled as the weather continued to cause problems. Work went on, drilling the ends of cracks and welding them up to minimise damage. One bright spot was a test on the double bottoms which showed that most of them could still be emptied. The helicopter continued to transfer material such as sand pumps, fuel and food to the hard-pressed salvage crew.

On the 14th of February the *Krab* came alongside and managed to connect up the after ground tackle which consisted of the same anchor and wire arrangement as the forward one. Once again the discharge of ore was resumed with the repaired sand pumps and hoses. Work continued throughout the 16th and 17th pumping out ore and water from various holds and emptying some of the ballast tanks. On the 18th a spell of better weather permitted divers to do an underwater inspection, which revealed a large crack some 55 feet long between holds 6 and 7 on the starboard side of the ship. The crack was located at the turn of the bilge. The *Krab* once again managed to come alongside and transferred the necessary fuel, food and salvage material.

Advantage was taken of the better weather to rig purchases to tension the ground tackle. During this operation the after 6-inch wire broke, which meant re-rigging the ground tackle. Work continued on the 19th and 20th at full speed with the object of making a refloating attempt on the 21st or 22nd if the weather continued to moderate. The tugs *Jacob van Heemsskerck* and *Willem Barendsz* arrived in the vicinity of the stranded ship during the evening of the 20th. On the 21st work went on pumping out the entire ship and pressurising the double bottoms. Towing connections were prepared on the foredeck of the stranded vessel for three tugs. During the evening, the tug *Cycloop* and the *Utrecht* arrived in the vicinity of the *Elwood Mead*, the latter now fitted up for pollution control. The *Krab* once again delivered fuel and material to the ship in preparation for the big effort to come on the following day.

At 0500 hours on the 23rd the ground tackle was brought to full tension and the tugs attempted to pull the vessel off, but without success. Another attempt was made during the p.m. high water but once again was unsuccessful, though the ship became lively and her head altered several degrees. The *Cycloop* sprayed chemicals on the oil which escaped from the fuel tanks, together with the water which was being deballasted.

On the 24th another attempt was made at about 0615 when the three tugs with gear attached to the ship worked up to full power. The vessel continued to work heavily, and grinding noises could be heard from the bottom plating in the vicinity of forward tanks and holds. At 0825 her bow started to move rapidly. By 0845 the ship appeared to be afloat in deep water. Operations were stopped. The *Gelderland* disconnected her towing line aft and the job of disconnecting the ground tackle started. As soon as this was completed the ship was moved towards the deep water channel, while those on board checked all compartments to make sure that none developed additional leaks. The *Krab* was left behind to recover the ground tackles, while the tugs *Jacob van Heemskerck*, *Utrecht* and *Willem Barendsz* towed the vessel away from Guernsey and towards Rotterdam, still a long way away. The tug *Gelderland* escorted the convoy and the *Cycloop* followed dealing with any oil that leaked out of the disabled ship.

By noon on the 26th of February she had been towed a distance of 203 miles from the point of stranding at approximately 4 knots. The ship was difficult to control as she had a displacement of 160,390 tons and her draft was over 73 feet forward and 67 feet aft. During the afternoon three helicopters arrived with men and more materials. Work went on checking the soundings and preserving engine room machinery. On the 27th the convoy arrived off the Hook of Holland and the tow was anchored in 120 feet of water. All the tugs disconnected and the *Utrecht* left to fetch the grab crane and barges which were intended to assist the vessel to lighten to a suitable draft for entry into the port of Rotterdam.

On the 28th, a floating crane was brought alongside the ship and her crew, who were brought out by helicopter, commenced rigging the crane. Unfortunately, on the 1st of March, the weather deteriorated, the crane barge broke from her moorings, and later the jib fell and broke in two pieces. The crane barge and empty cargo barges were towed back into port. On the 2nd of March, three air compressors were sent out to the ship by helicopter, and a pneumatic unit was connected onto the windlass to enable the anchor to be hove up. This was done, and the vessel moved to the vicinity of the buoy 'Euro 1'.

On the 3rd and 4th the weather was rough and prevented the heavy lift ship *Challenger 1* from putting four crawler cranes on board. On the 5th she returned to the *Elwood Mead* and using heavy duty pneumatic fenders managed to get alongside and place the four cranes and other material on board the ship. With the cranes secured, the discharge of cargo started at about 1400 hours and continued until 2210 on the 6th, when the draft was reduced forward from 73 feet 6 inches to 69 feet, and from 67 feet 3 inches aft to 66 feet 4 inches. At 2315 the anchor was weighed and the *Utrecht* commenced towing the ship towards the Hook of Holland.

Shortly afterwards the pilots and harbour officials arrived on board, and the vessel proceeded to the port. Unfortunately fog made it impossible to enter and the ship once again went to anchor.

At 2135 on the 7th of March, with the fog lifting and favourable tides, the ship entered the river escorted and towed by seven tugs. By 0400 on the 8th she was safely moored.

The discharge of the *Elwood Mead* was a long drawn-out affair, made increasingly difficult by the fact that it had to be done whilst moored to the buoys. In addition the increasing freeboard of the ship made it difficult for the cranes to function, and ultimately the ship had to be ballasted down. Work on ship's machinery continued and divers inspected the bottom and cut away some plating that was hanging down.

By the 26th of March the discharge of over 100,000 tons of cargo was safely completed. On 28th of March the ship moved into dry-dock for inspection and repair.

16   *Terushima Maru* –
port wreck removal

The Christmas or festive season of 1973 appears to have been quite disastrous from a maritime standpoint. The stranding of the *Elwood Mead* occurred in the Channel Islands on the 25th of December 1973. On the other side of the world, but just a day earlier, the *Terushima Maru*, a small Japanese log and general purpose carrier of 2994 G.R.T., was diverted to Singapore whilst on passage from Indonesia to Japan. The diversion was unfortunate as, on entering the Western Roads of Singapore Harbour, she collided with the Liberian ship *Isabella*.

The *Terushima Maru* was holed in her starboard side slightly aft of the transverse bulkhead between Nos. 1 and 2 holds. The little ship was loaded with a cargo of logs, and both 1 and 2 holds were full, with, in addition, a deck cargo of logs. The vessel listed quickly to starboard as the water rushed into the hold, and as she took on water, began to sink by the stern until the after end touched the bottom. The depth of water was approximately 80 feet, and after the stern touched bottom, the entrapped air and residual buoyancy of her cargo kept the bows above water for over sixty hours. Finally, on the 27th of December she sank completely and came to rest upright with her mast tops just above water. The hull itself lay parallel to the axis of the tidal stream which ran at up to 3 knots.

In a busy port such as Singapore, the wreck constituted a danger to navigation. The Port of Singapore Authority promptly marked it with a wreck buoy and closed the Western Quarantine Anchorage to shipping, issuing a navigational warning to this effect. The Authority also served notice on the owners requiring them to remove the wreck.

The *Terushima Maru* was built in Japan at Imabari Zosen in 1971. Her principal dimensions were as follows:

OAL	334 feet 6 inches
Beam	58 feet 7 inches
Depth	26 feet 9 inches

The loaded draft was 21 feet 5 inches with a corresponding freeboard of 5 feet 4 inches, and she was a standard design log carrier equipped with a 4-stroke, six-cylinder diesel which gave a service speed of 12.5 knots. The two cargo holds were served by two hatches and four 15-ton swinging derricks. Each hatch was approximately 90 feet by 27 feet 6 inches. The cargo stowage plans showed that the *Terushima Maru* was loaded with 1872 logs, of which approximately half were stowed on deck to a height of 12 feet.

At a depth of 80 feet the pressure of sea water is about 35 p.p.s.i. and this has the effect of reducing the volume of trapped air in the hull. In compartments filled, or partly filled, with fuel oil, the air and oil tend to escape through vent pipes and to be gradually replaced by water. The underwriters arranged for divers from the Fukado Salvage Co. Ltd. of Osaka to seal off the bunker tanks and thus prevent pollution occurring from the leaking oil. This work took approximately three days. The Singapore based salvage company, Selco, was awarded the salvage contract on the 28th of December, but work could not start until the owners and the underwriters had lodged bonds with the Port Authority to cover the costs of wreck removal and surety against any pollution.

On the 29th of December, responsibility for oil spill was passed from Fukado to Selco. Between the 29th of December and the 17th of January 1974, when the necessary guarantees and bonds were lodged with the Port Authority, work was confined to inspecting the wreck with divers, and planning the salvage operation. The main problem with a delay of this length is the damage done by salt water to the ship's machinery. Apart from that, it allows equipment to be mobilised and plans to be formulated. Selco knew from the reports of their salvage master and divers, that the vessel had finally settled on the bottom in an upright position. The deck cargo of logs was in place, and all the lashing appeared to be firm and correctly tensioned so there was little risk of the logs in the deck cargo breaking loose and floating to the surface.

Singapore has always been an important maritime centre. Since World War II, its importance has increased, as it lies on the direct route between the Persian Gulf, Suez Canal, India and the Far East. With the strong currents, shoals and heavy traffic in the Malacca Strait it was inevitable that Singapore should become a base for salvage companies. Selco, a local Singapore company, is strongly established. A member of the Pan-Electric Group, it has a number of salvage tugs and ships. Its particular strong point is probably the number of heavy lift vessels and floating cranes it operates.

Selco builds and operates its own vessels in its own shipyard. The facilities of such a shipyard are undoubtedly a major asset to a large salvage fleet and can, when occasion requires, modify or provide equipment at short notice. The company has carried out a number of very spectacular salvages on large ships including V.L.C.C.'s aground on reefs. From a technical standpoint it has also undertaken some remarkable jobs, of which three are included in this book. The *Terushima Maru* is a classic example of the removal of a wreck from deep water with her cargo in place.

No serious thought was given to removing the deck cargo prior to the salvage operation. It was well appreciated that letting the lashings go might cause logs to float to the surface and damage the underwater hulls, screws or rudders of salvage craft. Other problems were the current and the difficulty of collecting and storing the logs after recovery, and the possibility that the logs in the holds would force the hatches in an effort to float free if the deck cargo was moved. Calculations made by the underwriter's representative, using an S.G. 0.862, indicated that these logs would provide a buoyancy force equal to 700 tons. Selco using 0.871 obtained 660 tons, which was close enough to confirm the value of the logs in lifting the ship. It was calculated that, in the sunken condition, the two holds contained 4160 tons of water in addition to 908 logs. This quantity of water, together with that in the engine room, would eventually have to be pumped out if the vessel was to float free.

The collision damage in the starboard side was in the form of a 'V' shaped gash about 8 feet wide and 8 feet deep in way of frame Nos. 73 and 78. It was because this damage extended below the loaded waterline, that the ship took on water, listed and then sank. Temporary repairs to the damaged area would be necessary for the vessel to be floated free. The Selco salvage team were faced with planning the salvage operation and mobilisation of enough equipment and manpower to do the work.

The plan was to lift the vessel, using a combination of induced buoyancy and external lift provided by a number of salvage lift craft and pontoons. Examination of the ship's plans showed that she had four pairs of double bottoms, as well as fore and after peak tanks. The plan called for these tanks to be fitted with air connections and to have vent relief holes cut in the bottom. In this way it was calculated that about 800 tons of lift could be obtained.

"TERUSHIMA MARU"

CARGO QUANTITY AND DISPOSITION

NO. 1 — ON DECK : 478 LOGS = 1,083·58 CUBIC METRES.

NO. 1 —   HOLD : 420 LOGS = 1,572·52 CUBIC METRES.

NO. 2 — ON DECK : 486 LOGS = 1,075·0 CUBIC METRES.

NO. 2 —   HOLD : 488 LOGS = 1,794·15 CUBIC METRES.

TOTALS   1,872 LOGS = 5,525·34 CUBIC METRES

BROKEN STOWAGE

NO.1   HOLD   GRAIN CAPACITY = 3,758·48 CUBIC METRES

NO.1   HOLD   LOGS LOADED   = 1,572·52 CUBIC METRES

FREE SPACE   = 2,185·96 CUBIC METRES
OR 2210 LONG TONS WATER

NO. 2   HOLD   GRAIN CAPACITY = 3,731·79 CUBIC METRES

NO.2   HOLD   LOGS LOADED   = 1,794·15 CUBIC METRES

FREE SPACE   = 1,937·64 CUBIC METRES
OR 1,950 LONG TONS WATER

NO. 1 & 2 HOLDS GIVE TOTAL, 4,160 TONS WATER TO PUMP OUT

An additional 1240 tons of lift could be obtained from a combination of lifting craft and pontoons.

On this basis, the total lift available was:

i)   Induced buoyancy   800 tons
ii) External lift   1240 tons
iii) Log buoyancy   660 tons

Total lift   2700 tons

"TERUSHIMA MARU"
CAPSIZED AND SUNK IN WESTERN ROADS
24·12·73
(SURVEYED BY SALVAGE MASTER 25·12·73)

60 FEET

75 FEET

HOLE – 60 FT DOWN

MUD & SAND

300   250   200   150   100   50   0

POSITION : Pu. SEBAROK BEARING 189°(T.) x 1·56 MILES
LAT. 01° 13·4' NORTH.
LONG. 103° 48·7' EAST.

This was rather more than was required to lift a ship with a light displacement of 1945 tons, but some of the external lift could be dispensed with at a later stage if need be.

The authorities stipulated a deadline by which the wreck had to be removed. This was March the 17th (1974). It gave Selco only two months to do the job, as permission to start work was not given until the 17th of January. Because the salvage contract was signed on the basis of 'No Cure – No Pay', there was a very real risk that

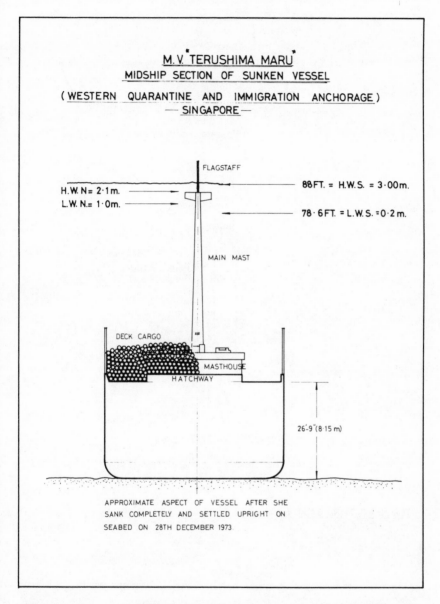

M.V. TERUSHIMA MARU
MIDSHIP SECTION OF SUNKEN VESSEL
(WESTERN QUARANTINE AND IMMIGRATION ANCHORAGE)
— SINGAPORE —

FLAGSTAFF

H.W.N= 2·1m.
L.W.N.= 1·0m.

88 FT. = H.W.S. = 3·00m.

78·6 FT. = L.W.S. = 0·2 m.

MAIN MAST

DECK CARGO

MASTHOUSE

HATCHWAY

26'-9" (8·15 m)

APPROXIMATE ASPECT OF VESSEL AFTER SHE
SANK COMPLETELY AND SETTLED UPRIGHT ON
SEABED ON 28TH DECEMBER 1973.

failure or delay would prove extremely expensive to Selco as there was no way they could recover costs in the advent of failure to make the deadline.

Selco had begun planning the salvage of the *Terushima Maru* on a speculative basis soon after the vessel sank. As Singapore is their home base, much of their equipment was ready to hand. The two lifting craft *LC3* and *LC4* were rigged and ready early in January. The motor salvage vessel *Salvista* was designated as

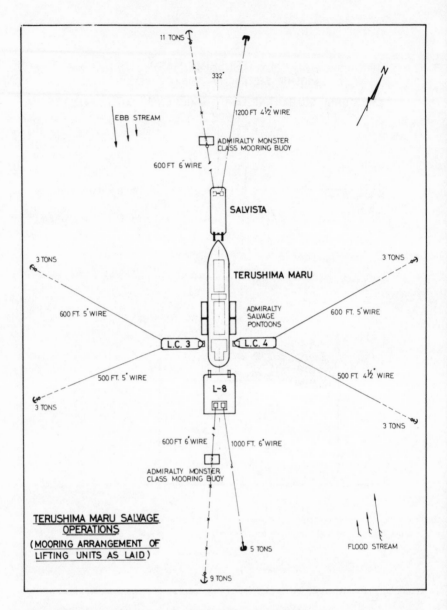

11 TONS

332°

EBB STREAM

1200 FT. 4½" WIRE

ADMIRALTY MONSTER
CLASS MOORING BUOY

600 FT. 6" WIRE

SALVISTA

3 TONS

TERUSHIMA MARU

3 TONS

600 FT. 5" WIRE

ADMIRALTY
SALVAGE
PONTOONS

600 FT. 5" WIRE

L.C. 3

L.C. 4

500 FT. 5" WIRE

500 FT. 4½" WIRE

3 TONS

L-8

3 TONS

600 FT. 6" WIRE

1000 FT. 6" WIRE

ADMIRALTY MONSTER
CLASS MOORING BUOY

TERUSHIMA MARU SALVAGE
OPERATIONS
(MOORING ARRANGEMENT OF
LIFTING UNITS AS LAID)

5 TONS

FLOOD STREAM

9 TONS

the operational base ship. Admiralty type salvage pontoons were
brought out of storage but only four were rigged instead of six as
originally planned.

As soon as permission was granted, the diving tenders moved
into position and moored close to the wreck. A number of jobs had
to be tackled by the divers. The fore and after peaks, as well as four
pairs of double bottoms, had to be fitted with air connections and
vent holes. Each tank had then to be tested to make sure the con-

nections did not blow out under pressure. On completion of the testing programme the air control manifold was secured on the *Terushima*'s after mast table, and the individual air hoses were secured so that they could not be damaged during the lifting operations. Divers had to remove the ship's anchors and chains to permit both hawsepipes to be fitted with slings for use by the lifting craft, and additional lashings were put on the deck cargo to make sure it stayed in place.

By the 28th of January, work had progressed sufficiently for the salvage craft to commence positioning. The first step required the lifting of the bows and forward section, so that the lifting slings could be passed under the ship. The *L8* positioned at the bows, and using the slings made fast through the hawsepipes, lifted the bows while the forepeak was blown to capacity. By gradually increasing the load, the bow was moved upwards. With the *L8* recording a load of 280 tons, the bow came up 9 feet.

Rigging heavy duty slings, wires and chains, continued for several days. By the 3rd of February the first pair of pontoons were secured in position, and by the 4th the second pair were in place and tensioned with 10 tons of buoyancy. Examination of the lifting plan shows the location of the two pairs of pontoons on either side of No. 2 hatch. The third pair were never used.

On the 11th of February the lifting barge *LC3* was positioned aft over the wreck's port side. Her moorings were run out by the attending tugs while the two 9-inch wires, which had been led under the ship, were secured over the bow lifting sheaves. On the 13th of February the four pontoons were blown to full buoyancy. By the 15th the *LC4* was in position on the starboard side facing the *LC3* and picked up the 9-inch wires. On the 18th, a test lift was carried out with the objective of making sure that all the lifting equipment and induced buoyancy, worked. The tests were satisfactory, and the heavy mooring system was laid to hold the salvaged ship and craft against the tide after the lift was completed.

The idea was to schedule the main attempt for the 24th of February, but on the 22nd, a Yugoslav ship stranded on Admiral Stellingwerfs Reef, 180 miles from Singapore. The ship was in an exposed position, and required urgent assistance. Selco decided that they had time to handle both operations. Unfortunately, the other units of the Selco fleet were also busy or under repair, so it was decided to send the *Salvista* and delay the lift.

The *Salvista* did not return until the 7th of March, but in the meantime a number of important ancillary tasks were undertaken.

The hole caused by the collision was fitted with a prefabricated steel patch. The engine room skylights were removed ready to enable the electrically operated submersible pumps to be plumbed into the engine room so that it could be pumped out without delay once the ship was lifted. It is a fact, however, that if it had not been necessary for the *Salvista* to depart, the operation could have been completed by the end of February.

On her return on the 7th, the plans were checked once again, and preparation was made for the lift to take place on the 11th of March. In addition, flat top barges and mobile cranes mounted on barges were put on standby. Water protection personnel from the Selco shipyard, led by an expert flown in from the United States, were also on standby.

The actual lift took place as planned on the 11th, and by 1400 on the same day, the vessel's funnel and bridge were clear of the water, and the forecastle and poop were awash. The *Terushima Maru* and the salvage fleet were moored to the heavy mooring to await the next slack water at 0930 on the 12th.

The location of all salvage lifting equipment and vessels is shown on the drawing, together with the induced and external lifts, as well as the moments. At 0730, the two large tugs *Salvixen* and *Salviper* connected their towing gear. Slightly later the smaller *Salvigour* and *Salviva* also made fast. The tugs held the salvage fleet and the tow against the last of the ebbtide before starting the tow to Pasir Panjong, about five miles away.

The vessel was grounded in 42 feet of water about one and a half hours before high water. At high water she was towed further up the beach, and came to rest on a sandy shelf. The *Salviper* was delegated to remove all the moorings from the Western Anchorage, which was reopened to shipping on the completion of this work at 1200 hours on the 14th of March. Discharge of the deck cargo was completed by noon on the 16th of March, and on the 17th she was moved further up the beach at high water. This operation was repeated on successive days, until the hatches were just awash at high water. Approximately 6000 tons of water was pumped out of the ship on the 20th, so that the vessel would float. Preservation of engine room machinery was started, and in the next few days, a great deal of cleaning up and pumping out work was done.

On the 25th the job was complete. By any standard, this was a well planned and executed operation. The Selco team-work was remarkable, and the detachment of the *Salvista* to go to the rescue of another ship was a measure of the confidence Selco had in their ability to beat the deadline. The ship was lifted with the cargo in place, and a full knowledge of the lifting loads and moments required. This was one of the biggest static lifts ever accomplished from such a depth.

17 The dredger *Mistral* in trouble

There are many types of dredgers in use around the world. They range from bucket dredgers, some of the older ones still powered by steam, to others, self-propelled and built to dredge sand and mud whilst actually underway. Suction cutter dredgers are designed as floating units which have to be towed from one job site to another. They are frequently quite big, and are essentially big floating power plants coupled to large pumps. Dredging is done by lowering a ladder to the bottom, on which is fitted a massive pipe. Inside the pipe is a revolving shaft with, on the end, a cutter which revolves, and will cut up the seabed including some types of rock.

The huge pumps remove the material and discharge it into barges or, if necessary, by means of a floating pipeline to the shore. Such dredgers are shifted around by using a system of anchors and wires, so that they can change position in a limited area. When actually working they tend to pivot around a spud, which is a heavy beam lowered to the bottom so that the end penetrates and fixes the position of the dredger. Using spuds, a dredger would move forward on a limited arc gradually cutting the seabed material away and removing it from the bottom.

A dredger is a relatively expensive unit, and is subject to considerable wear and tear, the pump impellers and cutter heads having frequently to be repaired and replaced. Other than the self-propelled ocean going suction type, the dredger needs calm seas in order to operate. Even in protected waters it can have stability problems, resulting from the misuse of spuds and the change in G.M. (metacentric height) when the heavy ladder is up or down. It is a well known joke among dredger masters that 'stability is not a wife and five children'.

A limited investigation done by Selco indicates that at least ten dredgers were the subject of salvage operations between 1963 and 1974. Selco themselves, were involved in two of these operations and therefore had some experience in this field when the Belgian dredger *Mistral* sank in Singapore at 0330 hours on the 25th of February 1975.

The dredger was known to have sunk on a shelving bottom with depths varying from 39 to 45 feet. A preliminary inspection revealed that she was lying on her starboard side, with the after port section awash, and that the salvage operation would be technically tricky if the equipment was not to be damaged during the operation. The lack of internal buoyancy spaces, the dredger's ladder and cutter – all added up to a major salvage problem.

Mistral was owned by Decloedt et Fils Soc. Anon, Brussels and, built in Holland in 1965, was classed as a suction cutter dredger with the following principal dimensions:

Length	164 feet
Beam	41 feet
Depth	12.3 feet
Draft	9.2 feet

She was equipped with two spuds, each weighing 48 tons, while the ladder and cutter weighed 60 tons. It was calculated that the displacement when she sank was 1491 tons, which meant that disallowing 100 tons for fuel and other fluids, the actual net weight to lift was 1391 tons. The Selco diving team who carried out the initial inspection, assisted the Regional Dredging Corporation (R.D.C.) staff to seal off the bunker tank vent and filling lines to prevent the oil from leaking out of the bunker tanks and causing pollution.

Later on the same day, Selco representatives visited R.D.C. to discuss the possible salvage of the *Mistral* and to obtain plans and information on the vessel so that a detailed salvage strategy could be worked out. Selco's experts came to the conclusion that the dredger could be salvaged. The plan was based on five stages.

i)   The removal of all excess weight, tools and equipment.

ii) The use of Selco floating equipment to turn the vessel upright.

iii) The lifting of the dredger by use of (a) A limited amount of induced buoyancy. (b) External lift supplied by a Selco salvage lift vessel.

iv)   The possible beaching and pumping out of the dredger.

v)   The refloating and redelivery of the dredger and its ancillary equipment to the owner, alongside the wharf in Singapore.

The plan allowed for the operation to take six to eight weeks. On the 1st of March the owners and their underwriters awarded the contract to Selco, in spite of stiff competition from other would-be salvors. The contract was on the basis of Lloyd's Open Form 'No Cure – No Pay'. As soon as the contract was awarded, the barge *Cosel-L46* was designated as the site operations control centre, and equipment was loaded ready for the forthcoming salvage operation. Permission from the Singapore Port Authority to proceed was not obtained until Monday the 3rd of March, when the *L46* was towed out of the base at Jurong by the *Salvictor* and was secured alongside the *Mistral* by 1220 hours.

The work of removing all the spare equipment and tools commenced. A large quantity of spares, anchors, wires, anchor booms and steel plates was removed during the next forty eight hours. The original plan to remove the pipe ladder and cutter head was abandoned after a meeting with R.D.C. engineering staff, and a discussion of the problems involved. Mr. Jerry de Jonge, the chief engineer of the dredger, attended the salvage operation on a daily basis, acting as the owner's representative and providing advice to the Selco salvage master.

On the 6th of March, the *Salviper* towed the *LC4* to the site, with the chains and slings on board, ready for the parbuckling operation. For those not familiar with this operation, parbuckling involves applying sufficient force or pull to change the posture of the wreck on the bottom. Once the centre of gravity has been changed sufficiently, the wreck then has to be restrained and lowered gently to settle on the bottom.

In this case, the *Salvista* and the *LC4* were to provide the 325 tons of pull required to right the *Mistral* while the *L8* controlled the rate at which the wreck was allowed to turn over and come to rest upright on the bottom. The control in such an operation is important, as hull damage and damage to plant in the dredger's engine room could result from allowing it to flop over at an uncontrolled rate. The *Salvista* was positioned on the 10th of March. On the 11th, the parbuckling chains and lift blocks were rigged together with the connecting pennants. One set was installed just abaft the main winch foundation area and the after set was led through the cross alleyway abaft the engine room.

Meanwhile the divers were busy fitting the air connections and watertight patches which had been fabricated to make the store-rooms suitable for use with compressed air. On the 20th of March a test was carried out between 0830 and 1030. Tanks were blown and the three vessels took the weight on their gear. Everything went very well and the salvage master felt that nothing had been overlooked. At 1105 the parbuckling operation began in earnest with the *LC4* and the *Salvista* pulling at maximum power and the *L8* controlling the gradual rotation of the dredge. (See Figure.)

It took 67 minutes to move the dredger and change its posture from lying on its starboard side, to the upright position. The dredger was rotated through an angle of 93 degrees. The maximum force recorded by the *L8* was 120 tons. Once the dredger was upright, the tanks were blown and the divers went down to survey the wreck for damage. Meanwhile, the salvage lift craft were recovering their gear and repositioning for the final lift.

The seamen who know the area, are aware of the strength of the tidal currents and the many shoals and reefs in the Singapore Harbour area. Some idea of the potential hazard is gained by comparing the same area at high and low water. In the latter case, a very much higher number of reefs and shoal areas are exposed to view. The seemingly innocent palm fringed islands are frequently exposed as part of a major complex system of reefs and channels through which the tidal streams swirl under the remote influence of the much greater water masses in the China Sea and Indian Ocean. The area in which the *Mistral* sank while engaged in reclamation work is known as Pulau Hantu, and is very restricted, so it was probably inevitable that the salvage craft touched bottom as they positioned themselves and laid out their ground tackle. Delays had to be accepted as much of the work could not be done when the current was running strongly.

On Tuesday the 25th of March, a test lift was undertaken with the *LC3* and *LC4* synchronising their winches on opposite sides of the dredge, and the *L8* lifting from aft. All air spaces were blown to capacity. A total lift of 570 tons was exerted by the three lift vessels, but due to the weight of the ladder and cutter, and some air leakage in the forward section of the dredger, no movement was achieved and the lift was abandoned. Another attempt was made on the 26th of March with the *Salvista* taking the weight of the ladder. This time the bows came up fairly easily, but again there

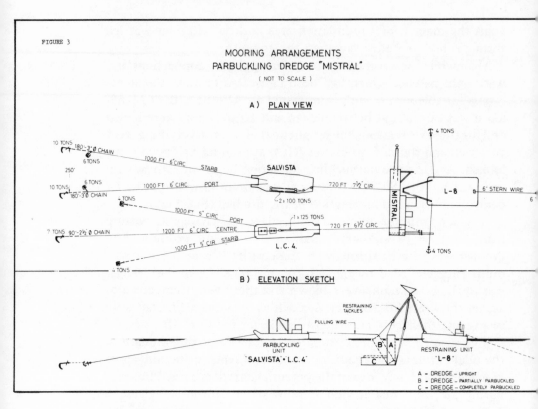

FIGURE 3

MOORING ARRANGEMENTS
PARBUCKLING DREDGE "MISTRAL"
(NOT TO SCALE)

A) PLAN VIEW

B) ELEVATION SKETCH

A – DREDGE – UPRIGHT
B – DREDGE – PARTIALLY PARBUCKLED
C – DREDGE – COMPLETELY PARBUCKLED

were definite air losses, and the wreck developed a 9 degree list. It was later discovered that air was leaking through an electrical conduit duct between the storeroom, which had been so carefully sealed, and other adjoining spaces. The salvage master had no option but to stop the operation, and the dredger was slowly lowered to the bottom again.

It was now apparent that the additional lift anticipated from induced buoyancy was not sufficient or dependable enough, and that there was no alternative to additional lift. After some discussion, it was decided to press the new salvage vessel *Salviking* into service. This vessel was fitting out in the builder's yard, but arrangements were made for her to be on site by the 28th of March.

The final arrangement for lifting the dredger consisted of five salvage lift craft, plus the barge *L37* which was loaded with ancillary equipment including a crane generator and pumps, to pump out the dredger once it was lifted to the surface. During the lifting operation the *L37* was positioned between the *Salviking* and the *LC3*. With this formidable array of equipment, the total lifting capacity was in the region of 1000 tons. The lift started at 1515 hours, but trouble was experienced with the *Salviking*'s winches. This took time to rectify, and the lift commenced in earnest at 1715. By 2000 hours, the *Mistral*'s main deck was awash and the pumping out operation started.

By 0130 on the 29th of March the dredger was floating freely, but was supported in the slings of the lifting craft while the internal spaces of the dredger were cleaned up, and work on machinery preservation started. On the 31st the slings were removed and the dredger moored alongside the *Salvista*, and on the 1st of April she was delivered at the Keppel Shipyard and the salvage agreement was terminated.

The salvage of the *Mistral* is remarkable in that the dredger really required a great deal of external lift force for a relatively small vessel. The use of five lift salvage craft and the coordination required, if not unique, is certainly testimony to the team-work of the Selco salvage crews.

18 The *Amagi Maru* on Helen Mar Reef

The islands and reefs in the immediate vicinity of Helen Mar Reef are reputed to be excellent hunting grounds for shells of all types and sizes, many of which have turned out to be collectors' items. Helen Mar Reef is on the Indonesian side of Singapore Main Strait, to the south east of Raffles Lighthouse. It is in an area where the currents are strong and tend to be confused, due to the junction of the Phillip Channel with Main Strait and the deflective influence of the many islands and shoals in the area.

The Japanese motor vessel *Amagi Maru*, with a full cargo of pig iron, was on passage from Vishakhapatnam to Jakarta. On the 3rd of July 1977 this little log carrier called at Singapore for bunkers and stores and departed again on the same day. At 2330 hours she ran aground on Helen Mar Reef, with the Helen Mar Lighthouse bearing 123° True, distance some 400 feet. Unfortunately the ship stranded 45 minutes before the highest spring tide in July 1977, with a tidal rise of 3.2 metres (11 feet).

The master took action immediately to refloat the vessel. Going full speed astern, he pumped overboard 155 tons of fresh water. All his efforts were unsuccessful, and in due course he began to appreciate that assistance would be required to refloat the ship. The ship's owners, time charterers and Singapore agents were informed of the casualty. Selco received word of the grounding at 0903 on the 4th of July 1977. At 0930 the tug *Salversatile* departed from her moorings, and at 1015 received permission to enter Indonesian waters. At 1100 the tug was secured alongside the stranded ship, and by 1115 the master had signed Lloyd's standard form of salvage agreement.

The *Amagi Maru* was built in Japan in 1971. Principal dimensions were:

OAL	101.86 m.
Beam	16.46 m.
Depth	8.21 m.
Loaded draft	2.09 m.

With a six cylinder diesel engine, her maximum speed was 12.75 knots. The stranding of such a vessel is not normally the subject of much interest. In this particular case however there were a number of complications, and from the technical standpoint the salvage was a classic example of the correct use of ground tackle.

The owners and time charterers, and the ship's and cargo under-writers, did not appear to be working together. The time charterers entered into a salvage agreement with Fukado Salvage K.K. Tokyo to refloat the vessel using the tug *Nikko*. So that from the legal standpoint there was an interesting situation, with the time char-terer and the owners' representative, i.e. the master, signing an agreement with a different salvage company. This situation was the cause of a lot of lost time, and Selco did not get a clear-cut go ahead until 1150 hours on the 5th of July when a message in Japanese, appointing Selco as salvage contractor, was received by the master from his owners.

The second factor of interest was that Selco arranged for a full diving survey. In addition, a sounding plan was prepared by the divers from the *Salvirile*. The ship had obviously run aground at full speed and was embedded in dead coral for about half her length. At low water the reef dried out level with the after end of No. 1 hold. A copy of this survey was handed to the master by Captain Hancox of Selco, who explained that the ship was unlikely to come off as a result of towage with one or more tugs. Not un-naturally, the master did not want to believe this, as the alternative of lightering pig iron and laying ground tackle would be expensive and time consuming. It is also possible that the Fukado Salvage staff may have buoyed up his hopes that tug power alone would get the ship off.

The simple facts showed that stranding so near high water on a spring tide, some 1000 tons of cargo would have to be removed as the ship was 3.0 metres out of draft forward. Largely to satisfy the master, Captain Hancox agreed to try tug towing power alone. This was done after all the legal problems were resolved, to take advantage of the next high water. The tugs *Salvotex*, *Salvirile*, and *Salversatile* made the attempt at 1435 on the 5th of July when the predicted tide gave a rise of about 3.0 metres. As anticipated by Selco, the attempt ended in failure and illustrated the futility of attempting to tow off in such conditions.

A second attempt was made at 0035 on the 6th of July. This attempt also failed, though it continued until 0420. During this attempt, the *Salversatile*'s towing gear parted, and trouble was

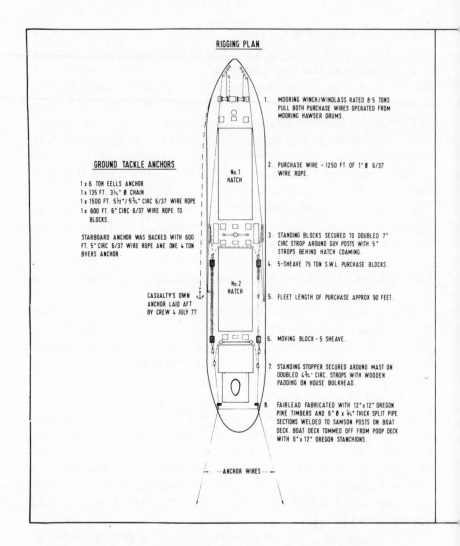

RIGGING PLAN

GROUND TACKLE ANCHORS

1 x 6 TON EELLS ANCHOR
1 x 135 FT. 3¼" Ø CHAIN
1 x 1500 FT. 5½"/5¾" CIRC 6/37 WIRE ROPE
1 x 600 FT. 6" CIRC 6/37 WIRE ROPE TO
   BLOCKS.

STARBOARD ANCHOR WAS BACKED WITH 600
FT. 5" CIRC 6/37 WIRE ROPE ANE ONE 4 TON
BYERS ANCHOR.

CASUALTY'S OWN
ANCHOR LAID AFT
BY CREW 4 JULY 77

No.1
HATCH

No.2
HATCH

1. MOORING WINCH/WINDLASS RATED 8·5 TONS
    PULL BOTH PURCHASE WIRES OPERATED FROM
    MOORING HAWSER DRUMS.

2. PURCHASE WIRE - 1250 FT. OF 1" Ø 6/37
    WIRE ROPE.

3. STANDING BLOCKS SECURED TO DOUBLED 7"
    CIRC STROP AROUND GUY POSTS WITH 5"
    STROPS BEHIND HATCH COAMING.

4. 5-SHEAVE 75 TON S.W.L. PURCHASE BLOCKS.

5. FLEET LENGTH OF PURCHASE APPROX 90 FEET.

6. MOVING BLOCK - 5 SHEAVE.

7. STANDING STOPPER SECURED AROUND MAST ON
    DOUBLED 4¾" CIRC. STROPS WITH WOODEN
    PADDING ON HOUSE BULKHEAD.

8. FAIRLEAD FABRICATED WITH 12" x 12" OREGON
    PINE TIMBERS AND 6" Ø x ¾" THICK SPLIT PIPE
    SECTIONS WELDED TO SAMSON POSTS ON BOAT
    DECK. BOAT DECK TOMMED OFF FROM POOP DECK
    WITH 6" x 12" OREGON STANCHIONS.

— ANCHOR WIRES —

experienced reconnecting due to the strong current, but by now the master was reconciled to lightering cargo. Meanwhile, Selco had made arrangements for barges to be sent from Singapore to lighten the cargo. The salvage vessel *Salviper*, equipped with ground tackle, anchored off the reef in close proximity to the stranded vessel. It was not really until the 6th that effective measures were put in hand to lighten the ship.

The first cargo barge arrived alongside at 0830. The ship's crew commenced opening hatches, while the salvage crews started to rig the ground tackles and test the dragline buckets with which it was intended to discharge the pig iron. By 1645 work had commenced on discharging the iron. The owner arranged for the crew to assist

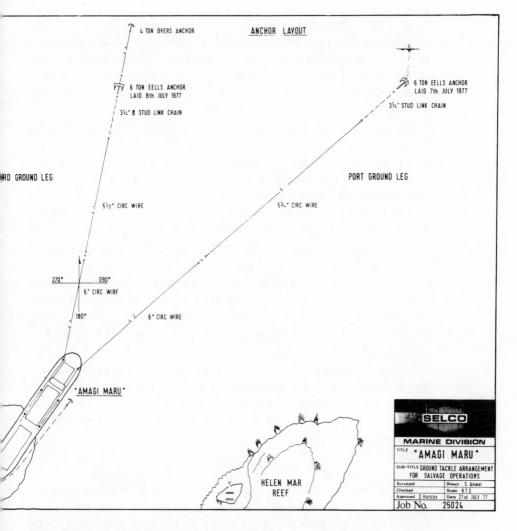

ANCHOR LAYOUT

4 TON BYERS ANCHOR

6 TON EELLS ANCHOR
LAID 8th. JULY 1977

3¼" Ø STUD LINK CHAIN

6 TON EELLS ANCHOR
LAID 7th. JULY 1977

3¼" STUD LINK CHAIN

'RD GROUND LEG

PORT GROUND LEG

5½" CIRC. WIRE

5¾" CIRC. WIRE

270°   090°
6" CIRC. WIRE

180°

6" CIRC. WIRE

"AMAGI MARU"

HELEN MAR
REEF

SELCO

MARINE DIVISION

TITLE "AMAGI MARU"

SUB-TITLE GROUND TACKLE ARRANGEMENT
FOR SALVAGE OPERATIONS

Surveyed		Drawn	S. Anwar
Checked		Scale	N.T.S
Approved	D. Hancox	Date	21st JULY. 77
Job No.		25024	

with discharging, and this was of great advantage to the salvage crews as they were unable initially to get stevedore assistance from Puolo Sambo or other Indonesian sources.

Pig iron is not the nicest of cargoes to handle at locations equipped to deal with it. In the conditions prevailing on board the stranded vessel, the ship's crew quickly became disenchanted with the work and the output slowed as the heat sapped the energy of all those working in the overheated and airless holds. By late evening on the 6th, the *Salviper*'s crew had completed rigging one of the ground tackles on the port quarter. The second leg on the starboard quarter was completed on the 7th of July. During the discharge of the cargo, a great deal of difficulty was experienced; the barge had to be turned end for end on a regular basis, and one or other of the tugs grounded at low speed whilst assisting this operation, as the tide was running strongly. The weight of pig iron on one side of the barge made it list dangerously unless it was turned regularly. On one occasion the barge broke loose during this turning operation and had to be retrieved.

There is a tendency to underrate the value of ground tackle. Admittedly it is a skilled job requiring the use of heavy blocks, wires and anchors. All too often the scope of wire or the weight of the anchors is inadequate, but when laid properly and used in conjunction with lightering and rising tides, it is an effective salvage tool and can be more effective than tug power. (See Rigging Plan.) Work continued through the 8th and 9th, and the ground tackle was hove tight at low water. By 2000 hours on the 9th it was calculated that about 750 tons of pig iron had been removed.

On the 10th, 130 tons of bunkers were transferred from tank Nos. 4 and 5 to the barge *SM1857*, and work continued discharging pig iron. The ground tackle was now put under heavy tension during low water, but some trouble was experienced with a foul anchor wire and retaining the tension. On the 11th of July at about 0935, the *Salvotex* took the fully laden barge in tow to Singapore, while the *Salvannon* and *Salviper* prepared to rig their towing gear in tandem for an attempt to pull the ship off at high water. This particular tide was predicted to give a rise of 2.4 metres, but the *Amagi Maru* showed no sign of movement in spite of the combined effort of the tugs.

During the morning of the 12th, the *Salviper* added a 4-ton anchor to the starboard leg of the ground tackle to improve its holding power. Meanwhile the *Salvotex* brought the next barge out from Singapore. This was the *Cosel L39*. Selco at last was able to obtain stevedores. The *Salvannon* ferried out a party of thirty stevedores, after a sustained effort by the local agent at Pu Sambo. With the ship's, and salvage crews, this meant three gangs were available to discharge pig iron into the barge. Work continued through the 13th and 14th of July, the intention being to make another refloating attempt on the 15th or 16th of July during high water.

Consistent with normal practice, at 1530, the time of predicted low water, the ground tackle was put under heavy tension once again. At about 2000 hours on the rising tide, the ship was felt to move and the ground tackle slacked with the blocks clattering on the deck, confirming that the ship had moved aft and relieved the tension on the tackles. At 2100 hours with the ship's engine going astern, the weight was taken on both tackles and the ship moved easily astern, and was soon clear of the reef, attended by the two tugs. At 2140 and 2155 respectively, the ground tackle was slipped and the *Amagi Maru* proceeded under her own power to anchor, well clear of the reef.

The *Salvannon* returned to Pu Sambo with the Indonesian stevedores, who were no longer required. At daylight on the 15th, the *Salviper* commenced recovering the ground tackle. A diving survey of the *Amagi Maru* revealed damaged bilge keels and dented plating, but surprisingly no leakage. At 1230 the ship received permission to proceed to Singapore, and weighed anchor. The *Salvannon* and *Salvotex* towed the *L39* back to Singapore, the *Cosel L39* having already been delivered to Singapore by the same two tugs earlier in the day.

Subsequently it was calculated that 2294 long tons of cargo, water and bunkers had been removed from the ship, of which 1841 long tons was cargo. Had the tides been equal to, or greater than, the one that the *Amagi Maru* grounded on, approximately half the quantity would have been required to refloat the ship.

The *Amagi Maru* reloaded her cargo by the 18th of July, and sailed for Djakarta on the same day at 1625. Captain Denny of the *Salviper* was responsible for laying the ground tackle and its successful use. The motivation of the crews and stevedores to remove such staggering quantities of pig iron, rests with Captain Hancox.

While it might have been possible to tip the ship by concentrating the discharge of pig iron from No. 1 hold, it would undoubtedly have induced severe hogging stresses, and this alone justified the discharge of additional cargo from No. 2 hold.

19 Oil rig *Orion* in trouble off Guernsey

Gales and storm force winds are not infrequent during the winter season in Northern Europe, but the winter of 1977–78 was particularly severe, with wind speeds of 90 to 100 m.p.h. recorded on several occasions around the storm lashed coasts of the British Isles and Northern France.

The German tug *Seefalke* was caught in one of these blows on February the 1st when towing the oil drilling rig *Orion* from Rotterdam to Brazil. The *Orion*, a jack-up rig, was mounted on the large ocean going barge *Federal 400-2* for the long journey. The rig was reported to have an insured value of U.S. $16,950,000, most of it secured on the London insurance market. The tug and tow had negotiated the narrow and crowded Straits of Dover in worsening weather conditions. As progress was made down Channel, conditions became more severe, with the tug burying her bows in huge waves which gradually reduced her speed and caused the westward progress to diminish to nothing.

On board the *Orion* and the barge the crew of thirty three felt helpless and uncomfortable as the barge rolled and heaved on the end of its tow line. Communication between the *Seefalke* and the tow was maintained by radio, and although a watch was kept on the heavy towing gear, everybody was aware that if it parted the chance of reconnection was small.

The English Channel is called 'La Manche' (The Sleeve) by the French. Technically it is a very appropriate description for this funnel-shaped stretch of water which connects the Atlantic with the North Sea. In westerly gales big seas are driven in by the wind from the deep waters of the Atlantic and forced into the restricted area of the English Channel. The gradual shelving of the seabed combined with the restricted sea room tends to make the seas particularly steep and dangerous. Strong tides add to the problem and can make the water look like a giant mill race when the tide is setting against the wind and sea.

In just such conditions the tow line parted, leaving the *Federal 400-2* adrift and at the mercy of the elements. The *Seefalke* made several desperate attempts to reconnect the line without success, and alerted shipping and the adjoining shore stations that the *Orion* was adrift some 20 miles to the north and west of Guernsey, and that they were attempting to reconnect. Ashore on Guernsey the Harbour Master put the lifeboat on alert and a French minesweeper south of Guernsey altered course and headed for the drifting rig.

At about 2100 hours on the 1st of February, the rig was just over 11 miles from the coast, and the tug master asked for a helicopter to take the crew off. He was told that help was on the way, and that two helicopters were being sent by the R.A.F. from Culdrose, Cornwall, and that a French helicopter had left Brest for Guernsey. The coastal tanker *Caernarvon* at anchor off St. Peter Port hove up her anchor and proceeded to sea, her master having offered to try to take the crew off.

Meanwhile, ashore, a mobile radar station was set up at Pleinmont and commenced to track the drifting barge and rig. The lifeboat was launched, and by 2150 was about a mile north of Platte Fougers and reported radio contact with the rig. At 2215 the radar showed that the rig was only 5 miles from the coast, and would soon be in shoal water. Soon after the *Seefalke* made a last desperate attempt to connect, and struck rocks twice, sustaining bottom damage which flooded the crew's accommodation and required continuous pumping to keep her afloat. The tug had to be led to shelter by the *Caernarvon*.

It was now obvious that the barge and rig would soon be ashore, and the lifeboat moved in towards the rig. At about 2250, the lifeboat actually got alongside, but there was some reluctance on the men's part to jump into the seemingly frail cockleshell. One man was literally snatched from the deck, and another recovered from the sea after misjudging his jump.

By 2300 the rig was drifting dangerously close to the rocks at the extremity of Grand Rocques and shortly afterwards, grounded. Watchers on the headland could see the rig and barge clearly, in spite of the spray and flying spindrift. Lit up like a large building, it appeared to move very slowly in spite of the pounding of the waves.

The roar of the breakers and the howling wind drowned out all other sound. Just before midnight the two R.A.F. Sea King rescue helicopters arrived, and one flew in close to the rig so that the pilot could take stock of the situation. Soon after rescue operations commenced, and all but six of the crew were winched to safety. While the second helicopter was hovering above, a dangerous situation developed. The tide swung the rig, putting the helicopter in a dangerous position and necessitating the suspension of the operation for the time being. The problem was that the helicopter could not keep position head to wind as it hovered over the rig because the movement of the barge brought the towering legs dangerously close to the hovering aircraft.

The six men left on the rig were told to keep warm and that they would be lifted to safety as soon as the helicopter returned. Meanwhile, the lifeboat returned to St. Peter Port and reached safety by 0415 on the 2nd February. Ashore, plans were made to remove the remaining men by breeches-buoy, and lines were fired over the rig, and the continuous belt from which the breeches-buoy was suspended was pulled across and secured on board. Two men were removed to safety by this means before the rising tide stopped the operation, making the rig move and endangering the lines to shore, which were taut one moment and slack the next. Shortly before 1100 one of the helicopters returned, and the four remaining men were winched to safety.

The skill of the helicopter pilots was remarkable, and it is due to them and their crews that twenty nine of the *Orion*'s crew were taken off safely, the lifeboat and the breeches-buoy saving two each. The rescue of the crew without loss of life was heart warming. All too often in the past, ships that stranded in such circumstances foundered with all hands.

News of the rig's problems was monitored by the Bureau Wijsmuller's radio watch in Ijmuiden. Management were notified and the tugs *Groningen* and *Biscay Sky* were ordered to the scene. The owners of the barge and the rig were contacted, and Wijsmuller offered their services on the basis of Lloyd's Open Form. Wijsmuller were aware that competition would be fierce, and the risk of the barge and rig being smashed to pieces by the weather before anything could be done, was a real one. Arrangements were made to fly a salvage inspector and team to Guernsey, and equipment and men were assembled ready to airlift direct to the island if Wijsmuller were awarded the contract.

Mr. Nan Halfweeg, who was on a trip to the Far East, was contacted in Japan and flew back to London, and from there to Guernsey where not so many years ago he had successfully salvaged the *Elwood Mead*. While Nan Halfweeg was flying back from Japan, Chris van der Zwan, Wijsmuller's commercial manager, was in contact with the owners of the rig and barge, and learned that a decision covering the award of the salvage would be made in

Guernsey after both had been inspected by the owners' representatives, together with experts from the Salvage Association and underwriters. He promptly made arrangements to fly to Guernsey with Mr. Cor Oudendijk and the salvage team.

Four companies were competing for the contract. Three Dutch and one British, and all their experts were flying into Guernsey to inspect the stranded barge and rig. Meanwhile, the storm had spent itself and the seas had grown calmer. The various salvage teams arrived and set up temporary headquarters in local hotels.

The barge and rig were boarded by various inspection teams using rubber boats, the Wijsmuller team including a diver and headed by Mr. Oudendijk made a careful inspection of the stranded barge. They found that the 19,000 ton rig had suffered very little damage, but the barge was a different story. The bottom had been badly damaged and several compartments were open to the sea. A careful inspection indicated that some compartments were still watertight, and it began to look as if the barge and rig could be floated off at high water on a spring tide. The problem was an old one. First, speed was essential or the motion induced by wave action at high water might cause further damage, while severe weather might cause the barge to collapse under the weight of the rig and pounding seas.

The Wijsmuller plan submitted to the owners and underwriters was based on the following facts:

1   They had the material, including compressors and men, ready to fly in as soon as the contract was signed.

2   Using a plan, they showed how the draft of the heavily laden barge could be reduced by induced buoyancy, provided by compressed air.

3   Based on Wijsmuller's calculations they felt that preparation could be completed and the barge floated off at a high water on the 10th of February.

4   Tow lines would be connected prior to the commencement of the refloating operation.

This plan was submitted with reasonable confidence as to the outcome. Their tugs were already standing off Guernsey and the equipment could be on the island a few hours after the contract was signed. Another factor in their favour was their record of achievement in the area with the successful salvage of the *President Garcia* and the epic of the *Elwood Mead*. Wijsmuller were finally awarded the contract, but the deliberations and formalities wasted several days.

Meanwhile, the Guernsey States Works Department rigged up floodlights which could be used to light up the rocks and beach area as well as the barge and rig. Arrangements were made for Wijsmuller to have the use of the large car park on the headland to stow salvage equipment which could be lifted aboard the barge. A Boeing 737 cargo jet left Schipol Airport in Holland with a load of equipment and men, which included compressors and pumps. A K.L.M. Sikorsky helicopter was chartered to lift the equipment on to the rig. Wijsmuller set up their headquarters in the Grand Rocques Hotel which was opened specially to accommodate them.

As men and equipment arrived, work started in spite of a force 5 wind and a lumpy sea that caused some motion at high water. Attempts were made to insert some heavy timbers under the inshore end of the barge to reduce the pounding. The helicopter made eleven trips to the rig and transferred ten compressors and other equipment, as well as a number of salvage personnel. Others used a rubber boat to make the short trip from the beach to the barge. There were only four days to go, and work went on all through the night. While a number of compartments were watertight, others were badly holed and rock had penetrated the bottom in several places. One of the rocks was projecting into the barge to a height of several feet.

It was accepted that there were major obstacles to floating the barge off with the rig in place. It was felt that the rocks might hold the barge in place and that sufficient induced buoyancy might not be available to lift the *Federal 400-2* off the rocks with the heavy rig in place. Alternative ideas were explored. If the barge could be shifted or made to take up a level posture on the bottom, the rig could jack itself up on its legs, thereby taking the weight off the barge, which could then be floated free. The rig could then be lowered and floated off at high water. Another idea was to turn the barge broadsides and cut away obstructions on the barge deck prior to pulling it off the deck at high water.

The actual attempt on the 10th of February to refloat the *Orion* and the barge on which it rested, was foiled by bad weather. Six men of the Wijsmuller salvage team left it too late, working against the clock and the weather, and they were trapped. A French rescue helicopter was called out, but was unable to get the men off, but the relief lifeboat from St. Peter Port made the wild trip to the rig and successfully rescued all six men.

The gale blew itself out, and the next day the men returned to the rig to find the barge badly damaged and in some danger of collapse. Another attempt was made to float it off using compressed air, and with the tugs pulling the barge round broadside to the line of pull. While the barge became lively, the attempt failed partly due to the poor visibility which hampered the tugs.

On the 15th of February a new plan was evolved by the Wijsmuller experts. This involved repairing the barge sufficiently so that, at or near high water, compressed air could be used to level the barge by providing sufficient induced buoyancy at the critical locations. This necessitated considerable repair work to the barge which was buckling under the load, and showing preliminary signs of a general break up. In addition, it would be necessary to blast the rock in predetermined locations so that the legs of the rig would have a firm stable base on which they could support the weight of the rig. The intention was to jack the rig up and free the barge from the rocks on which it was impaled by blasting. Once the barge was freed, the rig could be jacked up clear of wave action and lowered at a suitable time when the weather was good, and the tide big enough to allow it to be floated or pulled clear.

Arrangements were made for two explosives experts to be flown in, and permission was requested from the authorities for the controlled use of explosives. At the request of Wijsmuller, the owners of the rig sent a crew of twenty rig technicians including the barge engineer, David Metcalf, to help cut the welds which held the legs of the rig retracted in the spud cans. Work started on the rock outcrops, and holes were drilled in dangerous pinnacles to take the explosive charges. This work had to be done underwater, and the divers had to work whenever the swell, tide and current permitted.

On the 18th, one charge was detonated, but the weather caused this work to be delayed or postponed time and time again. Extra divers were flown in as the swell and current tugged and pulled, rapidly exhausting them. By Thursday the 24th, only one rock pinnacle remained. On Friday Theo Bosman gashed his forehead when trying to deal with this rock in marginal weather conditions. The 25th had originally been chosen as 'D-Day', but the weather once again forced the attempt to be abandoned.

The rig was now resting on the barge having been cut free. Its legs were free and had been lowered and jacked up again.

Everything now depended on getting the barge level. Time was running out. The 27th was the deadline, as this was the last day with high enough tides to float her off. After this day they would have to wait until the 8th of March before making another attempt. Mr. Cor Oudendijk managed to board the stranded rig on the 26th, and found that it was still in fairly good shape, but the barge had tilted and the rig was now resting precariously on it. The barge was in bad shape and it was obvious that it would not be long before the weather smashed it and toppled the 250 foot rig to destruction on the rocks.

Ashore, Cor Oudendijk and Nan Halfweeg listened to another weather forecast. A deep depression was moving in from the Atlantic – gale and storm force winds could be expected in a few days' time. After a meeting they decided to risk everything in a last desperate effort. Early on Monday morning, the 27th of February, the tug *Typhoon* (14,100 h.p.) and the *Groningen* (4,200 h.p.) connected their tow lines to the rig itself. When the tide was high enough, both tugs commenced putting a strain on towline, and gradually increased power.

In spite of the slight overhang of the rig's legs they intended to tear it off the barge by brute force as soon as the tide was high enough, both tugs commenced putting a strain on the tow line, and gradually increased power.

they saw it move. Inch by inch it slid and ground its way over the buckled deck of the barge, till all at once the giant legs tilted, and with the screech of rending metal the leviathan rig plummeted over the side, cascading water in all directions.

The jerk broke the *Typhoon*'s tow line and though afloat, the rear legs were snagged on the barge rail. The *Groningen* strained at the rig trying to pull it into deep water. The tug *Schotland* moved in to help the *Groningen* and finally it broke free, and the two tugs worked the rig further off shore. A close inspection revealed that the rig was not too badly damaged and was sufficiently seaworthy to make the trip to Cherbourg.

The *Orion* reached Cherbourg safely on the 28th of February where it was handed over to the owners' representatives. Back on Guernsey work went on trying to save the damaged barge and to get the salvage equipment to safety before the weather worsened.

The stranding of the rig *Orion* is interesting for many reasons. The efficiency of the helicopters as a rescue tool and the weather conditions under which they can operate, underlines their superiority to traditional methods in some circumstances. The use of helicopters to transfer heavy equipment to stranded vessels is not new, but the use of a large machine to lift great volumes of equipment illustrates its usefulness. Without it, how could the heavy lifts have been put aboard the rig?

From the technical standpoint, the salvage of the rig mounted piggy back on a barge is an interesting, if not unique problem. The use of induced buoyancy failed, and it is perhaps interesting that the success ratio with compressed air is much higher with tankers than other floating equipment. In the end, with time running out, brute force and a little luck succeeded where more precise scientific methods failed.

20 Salvage and the world of tomorrow

According to published statistics, marine accidents of all types are on the increase, giving an upward trend over twenty five years. This increase is due in part to the increasing number of ships of all sizes actually trading.

There are other factors, however. The speed of ships has increased considerably. The size and draft of modern vessels, particularly oil tankers, is such that lengths of over 1000 feet are commonplace and loaded drafts of over 70 feet are no longer exceptional. Crews are smaller in number and often not well trained. The cargo carried varies from passengers and livestock to complex machinery, and a whole range of manufactured goods, foodstuff and consumer products. Perhaps it is in the transport of oil and gas, as well as chemicals, that the most profound changes have taken place.

Where in all this, does the salvor and the salvage company stand? On the face of it, it appears likely that there will be as much salvage work as ever, but the equipment and type of work may change. Increased numbers of accidents make for a higher proportion of salvage jobs, but are the salvage companies and others equipped to handle major disasters involving new types of ships and special cargoes?

It is the author's opinion that most major companies are reasonably well equipped to handle the collision situation in terms of towage and the refloating of stranded ships. Far fewer companies have the equipment or the know-how to lift sunken vessels in medium and deep water. The industry has learned to handle oil tankers in trouble, and the dangers from oil and oil fires is much better understood today.

It has been proven repeatedly that the tanker is an 'ideal' ship for salvage work. Well equipped tugs and salvage ships can and have put out fires on blazing ships that have provided the press with spectacular pictures. The fires are frequently out in record time. U.L.C.C.'s and V.L.C.C.'s have been refloated when stranded, and towed into a safe port when disabled. *It is only in the area of escaping oil and sea pollution that salvage techniques fall well short of the acceptable.*

The author is aware of the problems involved in handling oil in the open sea when wave action, wind and current cause it to spread rapidly. Modern techniques are mainly aimed at containment and treatment if this is possible, and dispersal if it is not. The oil industry and the marine associated companies have never really addressed themselves to the problem seriously, and though TOVALOP and other schemes have been set up to finance the consequences of pollution from oil spills, little progress has been made in oil recovery equipment except for items like oil spill booms and small oil skimmers and separators. This is an area which should not be neglected by the salvor who is looking forward and not back.

Insurance companies and tanker owners should take into account oil recovery equipment when awarding such salvage contracts. Port authorities in most cases have strong views on the subject, and insist on this item getting a fairly high priority, when the work is in an area under their jurisdiction.

Another area where the salvage companies may need to rethink some of their ideas, is when handling chemical carriers that have got into trouble. On discussing this subject with the general manager of a fairly big salvage company, I was informed, surprisingly, that *the salvor cannot be expected to have the know-how and equipment to deal with complex chemicals and acids.* It would appear that the current *modus operandi* is to depend on the owner of the cargo for the know-how to deal with chemicals and also in some cases to provide special equipment.

Obviously having special equipment immediately available, just in case it may be used, is neither practical nor economic. Most bulk shipments of chemicals and acids are part of a regular pattern of trade, and their characteristics for handling could be tabulated fairly easily. Once this is done, contingency plans for handling such cargoes can be formulated, and the type of equipment which might be needed together with availability, could be listed against some future need. Many of the products handled in small liquid bulk carriers are extremely expensive, and some timely planning might be economically rewarding.

What about L.P.G. and L.N.G. carriers? Are these vessels beyond the capability of the modern salvage company if they get into trouble? Doubtless the stranded L.N.G. ship represents a valuable salvage job. A modern 125,000 M3 L.N.G. carrier costs over U.S.$150 million to build and the cargo is also worth several million dollars.

A stranded L.N.G. ship could, for example, have her cargo transshipped to another L.N.G. ship, though a special set of L.N.G. hoses or metal arms for liquid and vapour handling might be required. The vessel could then be inerted and floated off in the normal way. L.N.G. fire fighting courses are available to salvage companies who wish to train crews. A supply of liquid nitrogen and high speed foam must also be provided.

Unfortunately, L.N.G. and L.P.G. have attracted a lot of adverse publicity, *and some frantic and restrictive legislation*, much of it based on ignorance and the vague fear that ignorance begets.

The author has some experience of such ships and terminals, and believes that the L.N.G. ship needs careful handling because of its cargo, but there is no reason why fires cannot be put out and ship to ship transfers made possible if the need arose. L.P.G. ships are to a lesser extent receiving the same treatment as L.N.G. ships. Again, such ships and their cargoes need care and understanding. Ship to ship transfers are entirely possible with the right equipment. Salvage companies should look to their future needs in handling such salvage cases. Again forward planning might be a worthwhile economic exercise.

The salvage company has been discussed in terms of what the future may hold, but essentially the professional salvor is the casual servant of the insurance companies. It is with the insurance companies, not the shipowner that the successful salvor has a continuous relationship. How is this relationship likely to be affected by changing circumstances?

In the case of really big salvage jobs involving very expensive ships or special cargo, the tendency will be to place contracts with fewer and fewer large salvage companies, those that have financial backing to provide the equipment and know-how. To survive, smaller companies may have to combine resources or suffer failure, or take-over. Distance from the scene of the disaster is likely to mean less and less, and the larger companies will probably provide increased competition in areas which the smaller salvage outfits have found profitable in the past. In other words the trend in salvage is likely to be much the same as elsewhere in the business world. It is the view of a number of insurance underwriters that a reduction in the number of salvage companies is not necessarily in the interest of the individual ship owner or the insurance company, but most agree that there will be a trend to fewer and larger companies, and to placing more business with such companies.

Legislation on an international, national and port authority basis is likely to increase and restrict the freedom of salvor and salvage company. Much of it is necessary, some of it of marginal value, and a little, time wasting and expensive for all concerned.

There is a need for updating and applying on an international basis, fair and reasonable laws on salvage activities. The control of salvage work should not be subject to the varied influences of the inexpert local authority or those who have a vested interest which may be too narrow to meet the general need. *Salvage is a service ; the objective should be to legislate so that it can be effective.*

The success or failure of marine salvage depends on people and equipment, people being by far the more important ingredient. Men like Nan Halfweeg and David Hancox combine the qualities and experience to perform near miracles, but also have the judgement to know the impossible when they see it. Knowing the limitations of equipment and the individuals that go to make up a salvage team, is vital to success – team work and the exploiting of special skills of individuals at the right time and within the correct environment.

Modern equipment and having the right tools for the job is also important, but nature is sometimes of greater assistance than manmade tools. The misuse of equipment can be dangerous, and financially disastrous. Good advanced planning is essential. To plan successfully the planners need to know all the factors involved, and to weigh what has to be done in the light of available equipment and manpower. A successful salvage operation is, therefore, like many other ventures – to be successful it requires sound business judgement, modern equipment, good team work and a fair measure of luck.

Chapter No.	Page No.	Ships requiring assistance Dates	Vessels or craft used to provide salvage assistance	
3	14	1943 Cruiser H.M.S. *Glasgow* Freighter *City of Omaha*	Tugs	*Salvonia* *Empire Sampson*
3	14	Unknown Naval Drifter		
4	22	1949 Coaster *Success*	Tanker	*Esso Cadillac*
5	29	15th November 1958 Freighter *Nyon*	Tugs	*George V* *Beamish* *Simson* *Hector*
6	34	25th April 1962 Tanker *Olympic Thunder*	Tugs	*Holland* *Doggersbank* *Titan* *Simson* *Nestor*
7	37	25th November 1965 Tanker *Esso Deutschland*	Tanker Tugs Launch	*Esso Denmark* *Junior* *Cycloop* *Jebel*
8	46	11th December 1965 Tanker *Esso Peru*	Tugs Launch	*Cycloop* *Junior* *Delta*
9	55	24th November 1965 Freighter *Santa Kyriaki*	Tugs Salvage Vessel	*Titan* *Hector* *Simson* *Octopus*
10	67	18th September 1966 Tanker *Mare Nostrum*	Tug	*Friesland*
11	84	28th March 1966 Freighter *Bretagne*	Tugs Salvage Vessel	*Titan* *Nestor* *Octopus*
12	88	13th July 1967 Freighter *President Garcia*	Tugs Coasters	*William Barendsz* *Utrecht* *Stentor* *Teunika* *Irene*
13	98	18th March 1967 Tanker *Torrey Canyon*	Tugs	*Titan* *Utrecht* *Praia da Adraga*

Chapter No.	Page No.	Ships requiring assistance Dates	Vessels or craft used to provide salvage assistance	
14	103	3rd November 1968 Freighter *Etnefjell*	Tugs	*Groningen* *Utrecht*
15	109	25th December 1973 Ore Carrier *Elwood Mead*	Tugs	*Cycloop* *Utrecht* *Jacob van Heemskerck* *Gelderland* *William Barendsz*
			Salvage Vessel *Krab* Heavy Lift Ship *Challenger I* Unnamed crane, Barge and lighters	
16	120	24th December 1973 Log Carrier *Terushima Maru*	Tugs	*Salvigour* *Salviva* *Salvixen* *Salviper*
			Salvage Vessel *Salvista* Heavy Lift Barges *LC3, LC4, L8* Various lighters, cranes, pontoons and diving craft	
17	130	25th February 1975 Suction Cutter Dredger *Mistral*	Tugs	*Salvictor* *Salviper*
			Salvage Barge *Cosel-46* Heavy Lift Barges *LC3, LC4, L8* Salvage Ships *Salvista* *Salviking* Various other diving and small craft	
18	136	3rd July 1977 Pig Iron Freighter *Amagi Maru*	Tugs	*Salversatile* *Salvirile* *Salvotex*
			Salvage Vessel *Salviper* Various barges and equipment as well as diving craft	
19	142	1st February 1978 Oil Rig *Orion* and Barge *Federal 400-2*	Tugs	*Seefalke* *Groningen* *Typhoon* *Schotland*

Note: Helicopters used for transporting men and equipment have not been included.